What did you learn in the real world today?

The case of practicum in university education

Lars Bo Henriksen (ed)

AALBORG UNIVERSITY PRESS

What did you learn in the real world today?
Edited by Lars Bo Henriksen

© Aalborg University Press, 2013

Layout: akila / Kirsten Bach Larsen
Printed by Toptryk Grafisk ApS, 2013
ISBN: 978-87-7112-073-8

Published by:
Aalborg University Press
Skjernvej 4A, 2nd floor
9220 Aalborg
Denmark
Phone: (+45) 99407140
aauf@forlag.aau.dk
forlag.aau.dk

This book is financially supported by Department of Development and Planning, Aalborg University, Denmark.

All rights reserved. No part of this book may be reprinted or reproduced or utilized in any form or by any electronic, mechanical, or other means, now known or hereafter invented, including photocopying and recording, or in any information storage or retrieval system, without permission in writing from the publishers, except for reviews and short excerpts in scholarly publications.

AALBORG UNIVERSITET
PBL Akademi

United Nations
Educational, Scientific and
Cultural Organization

UNESCO Chair in
Problem Based Learning
Aalborg University, Denmark

Content

Preface	5
"What did you learn in the real world today?"	7
Epistemology and learning in practice	21
About the logic of practice	35
Praxis, PBL and the application of knowledge	49
Embodiment as the existential soil of practice. Philosophical reflections on the concept of practice as "doing"	69
PBL and stories of body in the hospital world	81
Inquiry in the swampy lowland	99
Engineering students in the real world - on-campus PBL	111
The Aalborg PBL model and employability	123
Lessons from the Euronet-PBL project	147
About the authors	161

Preface

Practice, praxis, traineeship, internship, or as I prefer, practicum, are all names for the specific arrangements where students from universities engage in real life experiences; in arrangements where they leave the secure tranquillity of the university and enter into the chaotic world of work. We, who contributed to this book, know that practicum is a very good way of learning, and it can be very interesting for all parties involved. The students like it, even if it is cumbersome, frustrating and requires a lot of work – work that is different from what they know from their previous encounters with the education system. In this book we ask a simple question in relation to practicum, paraphrasing Tom Paxton's song: "What did you learn in the real world today?" The question is asked without the irony of Paxton's original one. Neither are we indicating that the university is not real, but the question is simply asked in order to find out what is learned in the practicum. We know that the students learn and they learn a lot. But the question is what is learned. In the chapters in this book we try to shed some light on this simple question. And it turns out that there is no simple answer. We have confronted the question from philosophical and pedagogical perspectives and in addition to this we also investigated a number of cases.

In the chapters in this book we come across the terms practicum, praxis, internship or traineeship. These terms all carry different connotations and do not necessarily cover the same phenomena. What is common to these concepts is that they describe a situation where a university student spends some time, typically one semester outside the university. During this time the student performs certain tasks that are related to the specific field of study that they are part of. The idea is to replicate

Preface

future job situations and utilise what is learned at the university in a real working life situation. We also encounter the term PBL, or problem based learning. In relation to the theme of this book this could also be practice-based learning. No matter what the concept covers, it is still about confronting problems, with all the knowledge available and doing that in the context of the outside world. The point here is that the special arrangement studied in this book is an arrangement where the students work outside the university and – this is important – at the same time are studying their own practice. In most cases this means that the students are writing about and reflecting upon their experiences. Thereby the students learn, they solve problems, hopefully to the satisfaction of all parties involved and they write a report living up to the academic standards of the university. In this way the practicum is in no way jeopardising the academic standards and the practicum becomes an integrated part of the academic education.

In preparing the manuscript I owe a lot of thanks to the authors for their input and for their patience. Thanks also to all those students, company representatives and colleagues at the university who were ready and willing to share their experiences. Also a great many thanks to Victoria Wilmott for straightening out the language used. The entire project was financially supported by The UNESCO Chair in problem based learning at Aalborg University and by the PBL Academy, Aalborg University.

Nibe, January, 2013
Lars Bo Henriksen

Lars Bo Henriksen
David O'Donnell

"What did you learn in the real world today?"

A very long-lived prejudice informs us that university education is too theoretical and only partly prepares university candidates for their working lives in private and public organisations. Reading books and listening to lectures provides candidates with a lot of knowledge, but unfortunately not enough qualifications that could secure them a job after having graduated from university. It seems that this prejudice is confirmed in a recent report from The Danish Confederation of Professional Associations, AC. In this report (AC, 2010), it is argued that students with a relevant job during their study years will stand a far better chance of getting a job after their graduation from university. The AC-study also concluded that shorter or longer duration of the study period does not matter for the candidates' chances in the labour market.

Over a long period of time Danish governments have urged students to finish their studies as fast as possible; that is within the planned five years and not, as was once the custom, a prolonging of the duration of the studies. Candidates finishing their studies within five years as recommended, find it much harder to find their first job than their colleagues prolonging their studies because of working while studying. The reason for this, it is argued, is that relevant work during the study period is far more important, than the duration of the studies. It is further argued that grades are relatively unimportant when it comes to success in the labour market. That is, high grades are no guarantee of a job after graduation, but a relevant prior work experience is.

This report has spawned a debate on the relevance of the university education. Some say that the universities are far too theoretical and too concerned with life in the ivory tower; and not being able to equip the candidates with competencies relevant to the labour market. The universities were accused of failing to give the students what was termed dual competencies; that is theoretical competencies as well as practical competencies, which is thought to be missing or lacking in the present study programmes. All provide clear backing to the aforementioned prejudice.

The rector (vice chancellor) of Roskilde University, Ib Poulsen, responded to the critique by proposing that all university education should include elements of practicum or work placements in their educational programmes (Poulsen, 2010). Thereby the students would get the dual competencies demanded by certain critics, and they would be able to challenge the prejudice about university candidates and empirically prove the prejudice to be false. They could also concentrate on their studies and they would not have to work on other projects of little relevance to their speciality, and they should be able to complete their studies in an appropriate timeframe. In all, a proposal that would solve most of the problems pointed out in the AC-report.

The debate shows us that there is plenty of space for a discussion on university studies but it also shows us the forgetfulness of this type of debate. Earlier, in 2002, another report about the candidates from Roskilde University and from Aalborg University demonstrated that there were no such problems as a theory-practice divide and that candidates from Roskilde and Aalborg had no problems getting into the labour marked – more than one third of the more than six thousand respondents said that they had a job before graduation. The respondents confirmed though that practical experience was crucial for success in the labour market, but they also confirmed that they had obtained that experience during their university studies. Because of the PBL structure (Problem Based Learning) of the study programmes in both Aalborg and Roskilde the students get in contact with the outside world during the studies. Projects and cooperation with private and public enterprises secure the connection between theory and practice, and practicum placements often play a central role in this cooperation. So, on the basis of the 2002 report it can be concluded that practical experiences from real working life is important for the student's future career; and it can also be concluded that the PBL-structure of the study programmes of both Aalborg and Roskilde Universities is capable of bridging the supposed gap between university and labour market, between theory and practice. Therefore, on the basis of this report, the Roskilde rector was absolutely correct when he proposed practicum placements as a way of solving the practice problem.

A report published in 2007 concerning candidates from the humanities department at Aalborg University again confirmed all of this. One third of the Aalborg candidates had a job before graduation and 55% of the candidates said that they got their first job in connection with their master degree thesis and the cooperation with a company connected to the thesis. This again confirmed the importance of the connection to the labour market during the studies, but also that working with real life problems in connection to university projects and theses can bridge this supposed gap. Because there need not be a gap, universities need not be ivory towers and companies need not be a-theoretical. It is possible, through projects, for the university to meet and converse with the real life of companies. With the background in a PBL (Problem Based Learning) based pedagogic it is possible to solve the problem of the dual competencies and the Roskilde rector is absolutely correct when he points to practicum arrangements as parts of the solution. The question is now why the problem emerged in the first place; are the universities living in an ivory tower and is there really a gap between theory and practise? And secondly, could PBL really be a solution as suggested by the studies from 2002 and 2007? And if PBL is part of the solution, what is it that a PBL framework allows students to achieve and somehow bridge the supposed gap between theory and practise, and take this into their future careers. In order to explore and analyse these questions, and a few more that will emerge on the way, we present here some case stories of students in very successful practicum arrangements. These are real stories; lived in real organisational lifeworlds and academic settings. These case examples will, hopefully, shed some light on these questions and possibly raise even more interesting ones.

Cases of students in the real world
In the consultancy
We noted above how practicum has been proposed as a solution to some of the problems of university education. A student called Lene took part in the education programme with the official name Learning and Organisational Change. The programme is a two-year master's programme at Aalborg University, Department of Learning. The idea behind the programme is to give students with a bachelor degree, competencies in organisational change management. The programme is a two-year (4 semesters) programme, open to anyone with a bachelor degree (as part of the normal 3+2 structure of most study programmes at Danish universities). As part of the programme the students spend one

semester (in most cases the third semester) in close cooperation with a business company. The students are expected to make all arrangements concerning the contact to the company and the idea is that the student should prepare and implement a change process in a real life setting – a business company. Normally it is up to the students to establish the contact to the companies, but in Lene's case the contact to The Consultancy was established through the university supervisor, who knew the company through previous research assignments with the university. As the university supervisor also knew that Lene had a special interest in the areas that The Consultancy was working with, it was fairly easy to establish the contact. Lene found the company so interesting that she thought that the actual assignment was less important. She was sure that she would find something to do during her internship.

After having sent a written application to the managing director of The Consultancy, Lene was invited to a job interview. The company had a department servicing local municipalities and it was agreed that Lene should be part of this department for four months. It was also agreed that Lene should be paid for her internship and a letter of employment was signed. There was nothing in this letter about any assignment or task for Lene to take on, only an agreement on the duration of the internship. That meant that Lene were expected to meet at the departments office on a certain date, and the tasks that she should take on were to be agreed upon from that moment. Therefore she was unable to prepare anything for her internship. Instead she read everything she could get her hands on about The Consultancy and The Consultancy's products and services.

The idea was that Lene should work on an equal footing with the other consultants, but it became clear that this did not work as intended. The consultants maintained contacts to the costumers and the consultants helped the customers on very specific tasks, and they worked very individually, and did not involve others in their work - least of all Lene. Lene only participated in a few meetings and only as a secretary. At a meeting with the department manager, Lene told him about the frustrating situation and it was agreed that she should take on an assignment concerning evaluation of a series of training courses held by some of the department's consultants.

> Date 12:46, had a meeting with CS due to the frustrations I felt due to the lack of work and focus of the missing projects. It was a productive meeting where we reviewed the working paper I had made in relation to "The project active learning". It was

agreed that KS will make a draft and I will fill the holes and generally work more on it tomorrow, so it can be sent out tomorrow afternoon. We need to make a schedule, a presentation, an overview (Planning) and send out a request for a meeting. (From the logbook)

The idea was to make a status report and propose some possible improvements. Lene did some interviewing and it was found out that the customers had very well received the training courses, but the consultants were far from satisfied as they thought that they did not reach their audience the ways they had liked to. They also expressed some concerns for the courses, as they could not see ways of improving their training courses. Lene therefore started a series of interviews with representatives from the customers and with the consultants. This work was documented in a report to the management and the consultants in The Consultancy. During her internship Lene documented all meetings, tasks and her thought about the internship in general, in a logbook. The logbook also formed the basis for her final report for the university as well as the report for the company.

There was a problem, though, as the education for a master degree in organisational learning is concerned with, well, organisational learning. This was hardly reflected in the reports. Because the department manager, who also acted as the company supervisor, had a background in political theory, he was very interested in the political side of the matter and had no interest in any organisational learning. The supervisor from the university thought otherwise; he was very much concerned with organisational learning and therefore there was a discrepancy between the report made for the university and the report made for the company.

The work of Lene was very well received in the company. With Lene's work and her report it had been possible to revitalise a project that had been almost put to a halt. The consultants liked this, as the courses and the purpose of these courses had not been evaluated since 2004. With Lene's project it was possible to reconsider the aim of the courses and it was possible to rearrange the entire setup of the courses in question.

Data 13:23. Project ideas:
1   Analysis of cooperation in "The project active learning" - how to create a community of practice across teams.
2   Many costumers make demands on their employees that they must attend various courses. How, who and when - how to ensure the

quality of the courses. Is an extension of the evaluation of the courses necessary? How do you make them 'better' so that participants get more out of the product?

3   How important is the evaluation of the courses + questionnaire and the possibilities and limitations of participation (perhaps in relation to different forms of evaluation). (Inspiration found in Article: Evaluation as regulation of learning).
(From the logbook)

The university supervisor thought this was fine also, but he missed the organisational learning part of this, as there was only a very little about the learning processes of the consultants and of the department in general. Therefore the report partly missed the point when it comes to the educational goals as stated in study plans and the curriculum of the master programme in organisational learning.

Lene thinks this is due to the fact that she had not made a clear agreement with the company and the department manager before entering into the internship. With a clearer and more elaborated idea of the assignment she could have made a very good report on organisational learning in the department in The Consultancy, and she could easily have made this on the basis on the assignment that she got. But because of the political perspective of the department manager and because of the every day tasks she was delegated with in the department, the organisational learning aspect slipped more and more into the background. In terms of the assignment and the outcome of the internship – the evaluation of the courses - Lene's internship was a success. Also as a learning process it was successful, but in terms of a university report answering the demands of the study plan, there were some doubts, but not more than over all the semester had been an interesting experience – Lene had definitely learned a lot that was real.

At the incineration plant
Susanne had a background as a teacher and wanted to stay in a practicum arrangement in a business company, as she had previously worked on study projects with public sector organisations.

The company, Incineration Inc., is Denmark's largest waste management company. Incineration Inc. works on recycling and combustion of waste for energy production. Incineration Inc. has a department called Consumer Service that provides advice on proper waste management, and arranges courses for schoolchildren. Susanne was working in that department.

Susanne found the practicum placement through a friend, who has a family connection to the management of Incineration Inc. and it was decided that that Susanne should work on a project in consumer service; the idea was to integrate the personnel from the other departments in the visiting and teaching programmes of consumer service. Susanne's stay was in any respect a success, but there were some misunderstandings that could have been avoided or prevented. First it turned out that the company representatives did not have any idea of the purpose and the content of the education programme. The name of the programme is not at all informative and when Susanne appeared in the company it came as a surprise to some of the employees. Susanne also felt a bit confused, as she did not know in the beginning what to do and it was all left up to her.

Apart from some confusion the missing preparatory arrangement caused no problems, but a clearer description of the task and a written cooperation agreement would have made things clearer for all. Some initial discussions between student, university and company would definitely have been helpful.

The stay at the company went fine. Susanne completed her project and she was helped out by the contact person at the company and by the university supervisor. Susanne worked on a project seeking to involve employees from the other department in the visiting programmes of consumer service. So far there had been a kind of unwillingness, if not resistance, to doing this but through interviews with the different workgroups, through participation in meetings and so on, Susanne managed to develop a different understanding of the importance of having visitors and the underlying tension between the different workgroups gradually disappeared. "Now we can enter the control room without being looked at with suspicion" the company representative said. Previously there had been some animosity between the personnel working on the incineration plant and in the control room and the people from customer service. When customer service brought visitors to the control rooms or the plant the people working there felt that they were being overlooked or watched, and they did not like that. On the other hand the people from customer service did not trust the people from the control rooms to possess the ability to act as guides on the visiting tours, even if they are the people who know most about the plant. The customer service people did not think that the plant people were able to communicate with the visitors. Susanne's project was targeted at solving this tension between two groups of employees. She conducted interviews with both parties and arranged workshops and joint meetings with both parties. The workshops and the joint meetings were a huge success. The stories and the laughing at the meetings dissolved the tensions and it was possible for the parties to come to a mutual understanding, so both parties could do their jobs and respect one another while doing what they were supposed to do.

In all, this project was a great success in terms of results for the student and the company as well as in terms of academic achievements at the university. According to Susanne she learned a lot from cooperating with the company and the contact to the real world was very challenging and very interesting. She produced a 70 page report for the university which she handed in, in due time and defended successfully at the exam in January, 2010. So, this part, the academic part, was a success. The company part was equally successful as Susanne was able to assist the customer service department in solving some of their problems they had been working on for a while. After the practicum Susanne was hired on a temporary contract to help implement the projects she has been working on and when Susanne's present employment agreement will end the company is looking for other ways of employing her, due to the success of the cooperation.

To Susanne the contact to the company has been a very challenging but also very giving experience. She learned a lot. She had some reservations though. The study programme itself does not really fit the reality of the real world. The study programme wants the student to plan and execute a change, but it is doubtful to what degree it is possible for a university student to be able to execute a change in a private company. This is perhaps too ambitious as most companies would not have the students to manage a change themselves; or allow it. This is a task for the management, not for a visiting student.

The Company representative also found the contact a great success. The department got a new set of eyes to look at the problems they were facing. The extension of the practicum into a temporary employment contract proves this. The company representative would though have liked to be informed better before the practicum, and would have liked to see some kind of written agreement.

The university supervisor also found Susanne's practicum a great success. It is obvious that Susanne was granted the time necessary to fulfil her obligations to her studies. The written report was excellent and the presentation of the project at the oral examination was impressive. The practicum arrangement itself was also seemed a success. The missing preparations are, according to the university supervisor, not a problem – at least not for the academic part of the semester. It is part of the learning process that the student should be in the driver's seat and make all arrangements of the contact with the company. It is obvious though that the study in change management should obey the general rules of the university and make the written agreements necessary.

In all, all parties was very pleased with the result of the project, even if this project and the task given to the student was very difficult – negative stories and distrust is not necessarily something for students to handle – even seasoned consultants could have a hard time confronting such problems. But Susanne did very well – both in terms of her achievements during her stay, as well as in terms of her academic achievements at the university.

Shop floor layout in a machine factory

Martin was part of the bachelor programme in Industrial Engineering. The bachelor programme in Industrial Engineering is a seven-semester programme (3 and a half years) qualifying for the title diploma engineer. The programme is part of the Department of Production's portfolio of master and bachelor programmes. Choosing the bachelor programme means taking part in the compulsory practicum programme in the sixth semester. The purpose of the 6th semester is to complete the Bachelor education through a combination of courses, practicum and final dissertation. The purpose of the practicum is, according to the study programme, to give the students practical experience in working with the planning and implementation of engineering solutions by applying technical knowledge, management, operation and maintenance of technical installations.

Martin was twenty-nine years old and had a background as a banker and he had studied to become a pre-school teacher for some years before beginning his engineering studies. Martin was eager to get in contact with a manufacturing company and he started in late 2009 to send applications to various manufacturing companies, but this was unsuccessful. Through the fifth semester project he got in contact with Company D. Company D is a medium sized manufacturer of standard and specialised pumping solutions for marine and food industry, mainly employing highly specialised, skilled metal workers and engineers. As part of a 'lean project' where the factory layout was changed to a more rational layout, the company's stock and warehouse facilities were changed as well, so that they were able to respond rapidly to the needs of the manufacturing facilities. The project was initiated in order to enhance productivity and improve the workflow. Martin knew about Company D, because he had previously visited the company, but he knew nothing about the lean project before entering the practicum. It was agreed, though, that Martin should prepare, organise and implement the proposed changes in the stock and warehouse facilities throughout the entire layout, connected to the "lean" project, supervised and supported by the warehouse manager AJ.

The task was easily defined, as the agreement was focused on the new layout of the stock and warehouse facilities and their ability to support the workflow in the factory. The task for Martin was to assist warehouse manager AJ and participate in the planning and implementation of the changes in the warehouse. In addition to this Martin was also assigned to some jobs of his own, e.g. the planning and implementation of the new cleaning and degreasing facilities and plans for the best use of a heated and an unheated warehouse. Martin and warehouse manager AJ defined the tasks jointly.

The project was to be documented in a report, which also formed part of the basis for the 6th semester exam at the university. The report was supposed to include three parts; a description of the company (as a production engineer would do, with an emphasis on the manufacturing process). The task of the student (an analysis of the problems that the student was assigned to help solve) and the student's reflections on the assignment in general and the practicum experience particularly. To assist with all this, Martin kept a diary or logbook, as he supposed – very rightly – this would help him in the writing of the final report and it could form the basis for a future bachelor thesis (in the 7th semester). During the 20 weeks Martin met with his university supervisor once a month and every Friday with warehouse manager AJ, in order to discuss the progress of the project. These meetings were planned to last one hour, but normally exceeded this.

Martin learned a lot; especially the very difficult task of implementing changes in a real life setting which was a very interesting challenge, but could also be frustrating at times. Even if the changes were well planned, negotiated and discussed with the parties involved, unforeseen problems eventually occurred. According to Martin the university was not able to prepare him for that – it had to be tried and tested in the real world, in a practicum placement. This has very much to do with communication and communication skills, which are not part of the engineering curricula. In addition to this Martin found it very rewarding that the work he was doing was actually used by the company and was actually implemented in the real world. Martin found his practicum very interesting and very rewarding and he found that the things he had learned – theories and methods – could actually be put to use in the real world. Warehouse manager AJ was also very satisfied with the arrangement. He liked the work that Martin was doing and he is also very supportive of the idea of practicum in general.

What to make of it? – What does the practicum do?

Yes, practicum placements are possible ways of teaching university candidates. And yes, if the university is living in an ivory tower – which it sometimes does – and if there is a gap between theory and practice – which there sometimes is – then is a practicum arrangement a possible way out of these dilemmas? The students introduced above were all very pleased with the practicum placements – they liked it a lot as they learned a lot and they learned things that they could not have learned by staying at the university, even if most of the students had experienced some very challenging and sometimes frustrating situations in the real world. But that could be a necessary part of the challenging experience that is enhancing the learning of the students. They are placed in unknown and thereby challenging situations and they learn how to solve problems in real life and they learn that the knowledge they have gained through their education is able to assist them in solving problems in the real world.

But it is more than that, because it is not only a question of applying already acquired knowledge, it is also about the ability to find and create the knowledge necessary in a specific situation, in a specific context in time and place. This would call for another concept of knowledge as the students are not reproducing knowledge at some kind of exam output, but creating their own knowledge on the basis of the situation and on their previously acquired knowledge. When they are able to do that we are also concerned with phenomena such as self-esteem, reflexivity, and development of a professional identity. In the cases above all students produced a report for the university and in that report they reflected upon their experiences and it is clear that these reflections are an important part of the learning experience of the practicum arrangement. In all it can be concluded that the students like the practicum, even if it at times it can be very challenging. And it seems that practicum companies are equally pleased with the arrangements. They did learn from it as well and in most cases they got a new set of eyes on the everyday problems they were struggling with. Problems they would have had to handle at some stage, but did not really know what to do with. So in that respect it seems that the practicum arrangements were equally successful. Some of the students were even employed by the companies afterwards and what more could be asked in terms of dual qualifications and employability or dual competencies. The university supervisors also seem to be rather enthusiastic about the practicum. Reading the students reports is often much more interesting when the reports are based upon real world experiences. This is not just dry theory and reproduction of parts of the tradition, but it is a story about the real world put into perspective by the theory and it is theory used or applied as distinct from theory reproduced. This however does not mean that theory is under represented in the reports - on the contrary. In the cases mentioned above the students discussed theories of learning (e.g. Freire, Dewey), theories of language (Wittgenstein, Gadamer) or theories of organisational learning and organisational change. So the academic part of the learning experience is by no means jeopardised by the practicum, the academic level is just as high as in any other academic education and the students even get a chance to put the theories into use. The exams are therefore also much more challenging and therefore interesting. The exams are based on a written report and the report typically consists of an analysis of the problems encountered during the practicum, some theory development and of course some reflections on the practicum experience and the problem solving itself. The exams, therefore, take the form of a discussion between the students, the supervisor and the external examiner of the problems and problem solving described in the report. As for both supervisor and external examiner this is of course much more interesting than hearing a reproduction of theory.

From this, we may conclude that Ib Pouldsen was absolutely right when he pointed to practicum arrangements as a way of solving the problems of university candidates in the labour market. The practicum arrangements secure the students the dual competencies demanded in the AC report. It is able to bridge the supposed gap between theory and practise and it gets the university education, if in part, out of the ivory tower. But the analyses above also calls for a further investigation of the themes touched upon. It is obvious that the practicum placement challenges the students in different ways than class lecturers at the university would, or indeed could, do. That is, they would have to approach the learning situation in another way other than in the classroom. Therefore we would also have to conceptualise this form of learning in a different way.

If the students learn something else during the practicum semesters, the question would be what form would this type of knowledge take? How would it differ from traditional university teaching and learning? And how will the practicum affect the student? These questions are discussed in the chapters of this book. The concepts of praxis and learning are outlined further in the more philosophical and theoretical chapters and this is supplemented with case studies from the world outside the university.

In chapter 2 Pahuus investigates the relationship between epistemology, learning and praxis. This is explored within a historical and philosophical perspective. Learning is always about being with others and Pahuus introduces the concept mimetic learning, the learning from others which is obviously part of any practicum arrangement. This is followed by Zeller in chapter 3 where he delves further into the logic of practice. In chapter 4 the philosophical considerations are put to work. On the basis of the case study of an engineering student it is argued that the learning outcome of the practicum placement is different, but also much more relevant, for the engineer-to-be. Based on a hermeneutic understanding of learning a proposed replacing of the concept of learning as reproduction with a concept of learning as production, it is argued that praxis-learning equips the engineer-to-be with some necessary and indispensable knowledge that she cannot do without in her future career.

Practise, learning and interaction with the real world is a question of personal involvement; the students also take their bodies out of the university. Consequently, an analysis of the learning outcome of practicum has to include considerations of the body's role in the learning process. In chapter 5 Thøgersen discusses the problem of learning, practicum and the bodily aspects of the practicum learning process. This is further illustrated in chapter 6, where Botin takes the idea of the body's importance for learning into a concrete social setting; the hospital.

In chapter 7 Wiberg takes us to the swampy lowlands of the real world where the practicum takes place. With a point of departure in Dewey's work she shows how science and education can leave the laboratory and the classroom and be even more interesting when confronted with the world outside. This – inquiries in to the swampy lowlands - is - literally - illustrated in chapter 8 where Henriksen and Askehave describe how a group of students, in a case of on-campus practicum, helps a group of local residents investigate the annual floods of the area where they live, definitely swampy lowlands.

In chapter 8 we also describe the PBL (Problem Based Learning) model of Aalborg University. This model has, as mentioned above, proved very successful in terms of employability. One of the reasons for this success is the practicum, which allows the student to experience both worlds in terms of theory and practice, and in professional identity. In chapter 9 this success is analysed further where Krogh shows us how the PBL model affects the employability of the students and gives us some of the reasons for this model's success in terms of employability. In the final chapter we get an international perspective on practicum, when Kärmäräinen and Deitmer sum up the findings from the Euronet PBL programme – a research project investigating university students entering into the real world, from a European perspective.

References

Capacent Epinion, 2007. *Humanistundersøgelsen*. http://www.ac.dk/files/pdf/Humanistundersoegelsen-2007.pdf

Freire, Paulo, 1996. *Pedagogy of the Oppressed*. London: Penquin Books.

Kolmos, Anette & de Graaff, Erik, 2007. *Management of Change – Implementation of Problem-Based and Project-Based Learning in Engineering*. Sense Publishers.

Li, Huichun, 2010. *Organisation Change towards Problem Based Learning*. Aalborg University, Department of Development and Planning.

Poulsen, Ib, 2010. *Mere praktik, tak! (More practice, please!)*. Information, 21 April.

Rambøll Management Cunsulting, 2010. *Det frie valg eller det frie fald? – Overgangen fra studium til job*. AC. http://www.ac.dk/files/pdf/Det_frie_valg_eller_det_frie_fald.pdf

RUC & AAU, 2002. *Kandidatundersøgelsen*. http://survey.karriere.aau.dk/GetAsset.action?contentId=4045900&assetId=4045903

Mogens Pahuus

Epistemology and learning in practice

Introduction

At one time both epistemology and education were closely tied to practice. Epistemology was so to say an aspect of the development of practice, and education/training took place given that children and young people took part in the practical work and the life of the community. Then gradually epistemology has separated into particular institutions (the sciences broadly understood), just as education and training too have been made independent of practice (both occupation-practice and the social practice) and placed in other institutions (the educational system broadly understood). There is absolutely no doubt that this differentiation between the types of practice on one hand and the scientific and educational systems on the other, has been very justified. However, there has been and still is a danger of the differentiation resulting in too severe a separation, which is why the second time around it has been attempted to couple the differentiation with a co-operation, partly between the sciences and business and social life, partly between the educations and types of practice, and in the latter coupling certainly traineeship is an essential element.

In this article I first on a general theory of science level must argue for the fruitfulness of attaching both parts of epistemology and parts of the educations, to the various types of practice. Such a coupling makes possible that a new type of theories can be developed, which can be called personal theories because they relate to a specific situation, and it will strengthen also the personal element of theory development and learning alike.

In the second section occupation-practice is coupled with the more comprehensive life-practice, which it is situated within, and it is attempted to prove that this life-practice includes many different types and consequently also contains many different types of knowledge, which it is of importance to get part of. And precisely this is made possible through, among other things, traineeships.

In the third section – which to some degree is a unification of the first and second sections – the personal element in epistemology and learning is revisited, and it is attempted to concretise what role the personal – in the shape of, among others, the personal judgment and involved understanding – play in the studies, that are both a central element in much epistemology as well as a central element in many traineeships.

In connection to this I should also mention, that in this article I have had focus on epistemology and educational courses which concern the field 'working with people', in other words central parts of the humanistic sciences and social sciences and the educations and professions tied to these. I presume that some of what I point out is valid for all educations, wherein traineeships are included. But I simply have not considered to what extent my views are relevant for e.g. engineering students.

From practice to theory

There is an expression or saying that goes "There is nothing so practical as a good theory". It is found in one of Kurt Levin's articles on social science, but it is my guess that it is – the way it is most often used – connected with the perception most of us have of the natural sciences and the scientific theories, in that they have proven to be a decisive factor in the technological revolution of substantial parts of our (material) life-practice, which we all feel we are in the midst of. We believe – and to a considerable degree rightly so – that we can thank the scientific theories for a vastly improved working-practice and thus improved living conditions. That we on this field then, have a movement from theory to practice, which is valuable.

Precisely this relation between theory and practice in the natural sciences has meant partly, that other sciences and fields of knowledge have had a tendency to view the natural sciences and their theories as the more or less unattainable ideal, and partly the assumption that in order to improve the types of practice, which the humanistic sciences and the social sciences are associated with, one must work on producing good theories – in short, to think that here too the movement primarily goes from theory to practice. And it is indeed true, that theories within the field of human sciences can lead to an improved practice; just think of how a range of psychological theories have lead to an improved educational-practice. But at the same time two things can be questioned. First of all, it is not clear that theories within the field of human sciences are better – in the sense of improving practice – to the same extent that they hold the classic scientific theories exemplar. Secondly, it is not obvious that the movement within the field of human sciences primarily goes from theory to practice. It can be just as productive, when concerned with developing practice, to go from practice to theory – to create theories, which can enrich practice on the basis of practical experience.

My thesis in this section is, that there is a fruitful back and forth movement between theory and practice. The movement from theory to practice dominates at university, where students are presented with a range of single and cross-disciplinary theories that are to qualify practice, when one enters into this or returns to this. And the movement from practice to theory dominates during periods of traineeship, where one enters a concrete practice, that involves epistemological and learning processes and processes of change, and where on the basis of one's studies of and experience and familiarity with this practice must develop a type of theory, which for example will enable the students to design an epistemological course and course of change within this specific practice, that they subsequently have to test in practice.

Within theory of science the primary occupation has been with theories, that are developed from a logic of the subject or subjects in a certain distance from practice, however there are also reflections on a theory of science level on development of theory in practice. I shall begin by adding to Peter Jarvis, who in his book *Praktiker-forskeren* argues that theories, which are developed with a basis in practice, take on a very different character from traditional theories, that are developed from a logic of the subject.

He divides traditional theories into on one hand meta-theories, which are theories about aspects of a particular practice, when for example learning is viewed from a philosophical, sociological, psychological or financial discipline, and on the other hand theories about practice, i.e. more cross disciplinary theories about the actual educational-practice or nursing-practice. These traditional theories stand opposed to the theories that the practician or the practice-researcher develops in their practice, and which are personal theories, i.e. theories which concern the unique situation, that constantly change.

The latter theories can also be called theories in use – opposed to the traditional theories, which can then be called presumed theories.

Theories

Meta-theories (about practice)	Theories about practice	Personal theories
Philosophy, sociology, finance etc.	Single disciplinary	(developed by practitioners in their practice)
	Cross disciplinary	
	Integrated	
Presumed theories		Theories in use

When studying a very specific practice – something unique – it will be natural primarily to use qualitative methods. Quantitative methods can be used however, when the purpose is to compare the type of actors and the type of situation, that are involved in the concrete practice, with other types of activities and other types of situations within the same kind of practice.

A concrete practice is well suited for a case study, which can perfectly well be structured in a manner that deals with research and practice-change, i.e. action research, and which can perfectly well be carried out in co-operation with some practitioners on location, thus being characterised by collaborative research.

I agree with Jarvis that there is a personal element in epistemology, when this is based in practice – a personal element, which is also crucial for how, methodically speaking, theories are developed based on practice.

A common interpretation of epistemology – the inductive – supposes that the aim is to be as objective and unbiased as possible, when studying practice, and it is therefore believed to be essential to shed all preconceived notions – be free of theoretical assumptions – and merely acquire observations. This is the purely empirical way of thinking, also called the positivist.

An alternative interpretation – often called the hypothetical-deductive – says that no observations can even begin to be made without doing so from a number of assumptions, and it would be a pointless and unending task to describe practice without any form of theoretical assumptions. It is essential to take an active approach. To have been immersed in practice and have reflected upon it, and from the hereby achieved familiarity with practice to have formulated some assumptions about what constitutes the essentials of this practice, and thereupon move on to a more methodical and systematic study of practice, in order to disprove or confirm these assumptions. This is the more rationalist approach, and when emphasis is also on critically testing the assumptions, it then becomes critical rationalism. The latter way of thinking is also found in hermeneutics, which emphasise that it is always necessary to first form a general idea of the text – or in this case the situation or practice in question – in order to grasp the meaning of the text or practice. And a necessity to move back and forth between general ideas and concrete details, which results in a revised general idea, that is once more tested through observation of the details, and then again possibly revised. This is what is referred to as the hermeneutic circle. It is here interesting to note, that hermeneutics presumes that within a text – and (even if to a lesser extent) also within a practice – there exists a sort of essence, a unity in all the diversity; and seizing this unit is what it is all about – maybe the first time only through a hunch, an intuition – in order to rightly grasp the essentiality.

Following critical rationalism and hermeneutics then, the morale becomes, that the aim is to firstly make oneself as much as possible a participant and not just a distanced observer, when entering practice. Through this participation is acquired, to begin with, an unstructured general idea, which can then be structured through a more systematic and methodical study. It is also said, that here one has to be present with all of oneself, with all of one's ability to perceive and understand the situation. A more recent hermeneutician like Gadamer emphasises, that if one is not present in an involved manner, then the implicit assumptions, which are always present when encountering something human, cannot be tested. When faced with a practice, we bring along predetermined assumptions about how things are and should be, and only if we truly open up to the new practice and are committed and involved, can we have our pre-understanding, our horizon of understanding tested. Only by being actively and emotionally interested in reaching further, becoming wiser as to how practice should be – and thus in extension how life should be lived – can the encounter with practice become a true meeting, where oneself can change – and consequently also where shortcomings in one's pre-understanding can be made conscious and reformed. By trying to remain neutral and distanced, one is not made aware in the same manner that there is no absolute neutrality and one always brings along ways of thinking.

Types of practice and types of knowledge

The practice we have opposed to theory in the previous section is of course different types of occupation-practice, but it is important to be aware that such types of practice in turn are situated within a comprehensive life-practice. In this way three levels of practice are distinguishable, where the uppermost is the most specialised and the lowermost the least specialised:

Theoretical practice (science)
Occupation-practice
Life-practice

It was till now the point that there should preferably be a correlation between occupation-practice and theoretical practice. However, correspondingly there should also be a correlation between occupation-practice and life-practice. Both in order for occupation-practice to encompass 'the whole man', as well as for a trainee service within occupation-practice to be able to take advantage of the opportunities for learning attached to a traineeship. This will be evident through further description of the different types of practice and the associated types of knowledge that are included in life-practice:

1. The type of practice we first think of is probably work or the instrumental activity, where we process something natural into a product. In today's world work has to be generalised even further – that is to say what Habermas (in his *Theorie des kommunikativen Handelns*) calls goal-directed practice, which includes any form of goal oriented action where certain means are used to realise a new state of things (the goal).
2. This goal-directed practice is almost always coupled with another type of practice, namely joint-practice, interaction, which is ordinarily imparted through communication and thus – again using Habermas – can also be called communicative practice. Here one coordinates with other people (e.g. through making promises, through entering into agreements or contracts etc.), or go the step further and enter an actual working relationship. To both these types of practice is associated a type of knowledge, a type of rationality or reason,

which – again using Habermas – we can call cognitive-instrumental rationality and moral-practical rationality respectively.
3. It is possible – using Heidegger (in *Sein und* Zeit) and other phenomenologists – to say, that apart from standing in relation to the surrounding world (Umwelt) and in relation to others (Mitwelt) we also always relate us to ourselves (Eigenwelt). This relating to oneself can be described as primarily an attempt to clarify what moves in us (in terms of impulses, emotions etc.), and in extension hereof, an attempt to clarify how the different impulses within us should be assessed and weighted against one another. This type of action can – using Habermas – be called an expressive-aesthetic action, where we through the act of expressing (expressivity) clarify what moves in us, and where through this shaping of the inner world, which happens through the expression, we arrive at an assessment and weighting. To this type of action is associated a third type of understanding or reason that Habermas calls an expressive-aesthetic rationality, which can furthermore be separated into a therapeutic understanding (that does not take the form of a discourse, but of a critique) that aims at a clarification of what moves in us, and an artistic understanding or critique that aims to clarify how something internal should be assessed and weighted.
4. It is however possible to establish a further two types of action, that is (fourthly) a relation to the sensory perceptible, where we are engrossed in and dwell on the sensory for its own sake – an activity that consists of a primarily instinctive bodily imitation of the sensory, and which therefore can be called a bodily-mimetic activity.
5. And – fifthly – an activity where we are engaged in other people for their own sake and engaged in being with them for the social aspect's own sake. This we can – using Habermas – call the 'happy' communicative community. Also these two types of activity are connected with types of knowledge, namely empathic forms of perception and understanding.

I have here added to Habermas' conceptions of the different types of knowledge, but one can also compare with a range of other typologies for types of knowledge:

On an entirely general level it is possible to distinguish between two types of knowledge, namely theoretical knowledge (a form of knowledge that ties into theoretical practice, and which is characterised by 'know that' or propositional knowledge) and practical knowledge (a form of knowledge that ties into both occupation-practice and life-practice, and which – in supplement to propositional knowledge – is characterised by 'know how').

When talking about know-how the first thing that probably comes to mind is a type of knowledge that ties into the instrumental or goal-directed practice, but the concept actually also covers the communicative practice. And when going further and talking about practical knowledge as knowledge by acquaintance (and as tacit, personal and situated – unlike propositional knowledge, which is explicit, impersonal and context free) – then these concepts encompass the entire spectrum of the five types of activity that were listed earlier.

Comparing this with Aristotle's trichotomy of knowledge, episteme, phronesis and techne, it becomes clear that episteme corresponds to theoretical knowledge, while phronesis covers the knowledge that is tied to the communicative practice, and while techne covers partly the knowledge that is tied to instrumental action, and partly the knowledge we earlier referred to as therapeutic and artistic understanding, and which tied into the aesthetic-expressive action. Aristotle is in fact also aware of the form of empathic understanding that is tied to mimetic action. However, neither he nor other didactic thinkers, who had been aware of the importance of imitation for the development of understanding and proficiencies, had been attentive to the form of imitation, where one instinctively with one's body and one's movements imitate what other people do; and certainly not, that we also through this method get to know the surrounding world – that is to say, when we imitate other living beings' movements, indeed even imitating movements and efforts of the non-living nature. Let me further elaborate on this statement:

It is clear to anyone, that children with their postures and movements imitate the adults. But adults do the same thing – only without being aware of it. One of the places where it is possible to catch oneself doing this involuntary bodily imitation is in the theatre. If gripped by the actors' play, one will find that one's body has to be controlled in order to not all too obviously (and annoyingly for the rest of the audience) carry out an instinctive imitation of gestures and postures. But also in relation to animals we imitate. This is sensed clearly when visiting a zoo, where animals with completely different and unaccustomed to movement patterns are encountered. From here we can move on to the experience of trees, where, to a greater degree than one would think, trees are perceived and 'understood' by stretching one's body out and up in varying ways (as the trunk does) – and stretching oneself outward (as the branches) and carry (as the crown) and float (as the new leaf). And from here we can finally move on to the non-living nature, and discover that in our perception of the undulating hilly country we activate our own bodily rhythmic movements. Just as in our perception of the surf we follow the waves breaking with a perceptible, but fairly invisible, bodily breaking, and finally, just as we perceive the mountains with our own bodily mountainous rising.

It is this entire register of practical knowledge and practical understanding that students to a greater degree get access to and develop, when they leave the institutions and enter into a traineeship. Provided of course, that occupation-practice is not too one-sidedly inclined to merely consist of instrumental practice. Previously many forms of occupation-practice had quite the one-sided disposition (assembly line work, monotonous work), but most modern forms of occupation-practice are certainly richer – and include many aspects of life-practice.

The personal element in the development of knowledge in practice

So far however, it is far from all types of occupation-practice that include all types of life-practice and the associated forms of understanding, and which therefore do not develop what we call 'the whole man'. But it is possible to establish it as a goal for both occupation-practice – and to the traineeship's associated way of developing one's knowledge – that the aim is to utilise all of oneself, which again means that the aim is not only to activate the aspects of oneself in the below arrangement, which are in the column to the left, but also the complimentary capacities in the column to the right:

The intellectual	The emotional
Handling, mastering	That an activity comes naturally, flow, keenness
Determination	Openness and unfocusing
Skill	Life
Character traits	Nature, being
Performing, playing parts	Being oneself (unforced, free, spontaneous)

In by far the most educations – and in by far the most businesses – it is the capacities in the left column that are prioritised at the expense and neglect of the capacities in the right column. But even though the two columns imply a sort of contradiction, they are however combinable into something integrated. When, for example, handling is combined with the spontaneous energies from the right side, it results in managing; and we all know that it is better to manage your job than simply to handle it (perhaps barely and only with great effort, and perhaps with stress as a result). When determination is combined with the open and receptive from the right side, it results in attentiveness; and everyone knows from their own experience, that an attentive teacher, who you feel sees you as the person you are, has a much greater significance for your development than the merely determined teacher has.

Let us now – with the acknowledgement that there are many types of life-practice and associated types of knowledge and understanding, not least an emotional and empathic one – return to the question of how to more concretely include the personal element in human epistemology in relation to practice.

Let us take the example that one wishes to examine how it feels to be incurably ill. Well, here it would be natural to use the interview method, which is a type of qualitative method, a method which will yield a series of data in the shape of a number of taped or possibly transcribed interviews. This data has to be analysed, and the analysis is rather methodical, however there is also a need for three elements in the process, which are not analysis and which are not carried out in a methodical manner, but which precisely has a more personal character.

In the preliminary phase, where one contemplates which questions to ask during the interviews, the aim is to try and identify oneself as much as possible with the situation of having been told that you are incurably ill. Here it is necessary to use one's imagination in a free and uncontrolled fashion, in order to get a sense of which questions it will be relevant to ask. It is of course also possible to stimulate one's own imagination, through reading accounts by incurably ill or through reading fictional descriptions of people who are in such a situation. Finally, it is also possible to sit down and do a philosophical analysis of the situation of the incurably ill – on a basis of sympathetic insight into said situation. Such a phenomenological analysis consists after all of "drawing forth the understanding of human nature and worldly conditions, which lie hidden in the pre-philosophical knowledge" (Løgstrup, 1987, p. 117), where the pre-philosophical knowledge is the understanding of the type of situation, which we have from our own life and the life of others. In this way one's pre-understandings of this type of situation is made aware, before going into the actual interview situation. Such a pre-understanding is primarily a practical knowledge – of the intimacy type, and contains elements of both aesthetic-expressive understanding and empathic understanding. On the basis hereof it is possible to structure the interview in advance. Then, as one begins with each separate interview, it is necessary to constantly be attentive to whether the interviewee brings something into the conversation that is completely unexpected – an attentiveness which again has the traits of aesthetic-expressive and empathic understanding. If this is the case, then one has to be able to change the pre-structuralisation of the interview on the fly, in order to immerse oneself in the new and unexpected. This is the second element in the uncontrolled and personal.

The third element then comes into play, when reading through all the interviews. Here the aim, through as an involved reading as possible – is involved in the sense that all aspects of oneself are used, both the capacity for thought, emotions and imagination, in a non-controllable manner – to form an overview of what is central to both each single interviewees' experience of this situation, and – on a higher level – whether what is central for the first person is the same as what is central for the subsequent interviewees, or if it is necessary to operate with different ways of experiencing the situation.

Only here does the actual methodical work begin. After having formed an overview of the single interview and the collected interviews, it is necessary to verify whether one's interpretation holds true. Is one's general impression verified by the single interview, when it is analysed by dividing it into themes and subthemes through meticulously registering which words and concepts the person uses etc.? And do the collected interviews confirm the assumption that there exists a range of different typical ways in which to experience the situation?

If one wants to examine the interplay between the incurably ill, his or her spouse and nursing staff – e.g. to discover what characterises the successful interplay in relation to the unsuccessful interplay – then it would be reasonable to make use of observation (possibly participant observation), perhaps in addition to interviews with the three parties. Here the data will be a series of field notes or audio/video recordings, which again are possibly printed and transcribed. Here too, in relation to the analysis of this kind of material, there are elements that are not analysis. To begin with, it is once more a good idea to use oneself and one's empathy and imagination in order to get an idea of what you would want from this interplay, if you were in that situation. Thus you are better equipped to make observations and take notes. During the process one has to revise this pre-understanding every time something unexpected occurs. And once more it is at the end necessary to read through the notes with everything one has – and in an involved, sympathetic way, in order to formulate a general view of the successful interplay and of the unsuccessful interplay (or of the different forms of both parts). And again the actual analysis becomes an examination of whether one's understanding of the whole holds true or not.

It is important to understand that in encountering life-practice one always has a pre-understanding. The only question is whether this will be allowed to remain on an unconscious and ill-considered level, where parts of the pre-understanding are made up of popular prejudices, or if they will be made conscious – in preparation of testing them. One may think, that the empirical material itself invites conceptualisation – coding as it is called in grounded theory – but in my opinion it will just as much be the non-conscious pre-understanding, that delivers the concepts.

It is just as important to understand – and here I return to the discussion of the inductive as opposed to the hypothetico-deductive method – that we must always employ an alternation between an understanding of the whole and an understanding of elements/details.

To the inductivists, who believe that an understanding of the whole – e.g. the central category referred to in grounded theory – has to arise from all the elements (the details) and to the deductivists, who believe that we have to begin with the already established scientific theories and concepts, and from there move on to empiricism, I will recommend diving into the empirical material. Diving in with everything one has, with all the multible forms of understanding that were lined up in the section about types of practice and types of knowledge, through such a dive to emerge with an understanding of the whole, an understanding of core and centre – and then testing this understanding of the whole through an analysis of the details, where it will always be the case that the details will refer to a revision of the understanding of the whole, which in its revised form is then tested through a new examination of details etc.

References

Habermas, Jürgen, 1972. *Theorie des kommunikativen Handelns I-II.* Frankfurt am Main. Suhrkamp.

Heidegger, Martin, 1974. *Sein und Zeit.* Tübingen. Max Niemeyer Verlag.

Jarvis, Peter, 2002. *Praktiker-forskeren. (Practitioner-researcher).* København. Forlaget Alenea.

Løgstrup, K. E., 1987. *Solidaritet og kærlighed. (Solidarity and love).* København, Gyldendal,

Jörg Zeller

About the logic of practice

Introduction
Practice is the way humans try to make the world, that nobody has had a chance to accept or deny before being born, meaningful and valuable. We can be lucky and meet the world equipped with favourable conditions to make it even better; or we can be less fortunate having to fight from the very beginning just for survival, not to mention for happiness and a good life. Having a broad spectrum of practices, which people try to learn and develop in order to cope with the challenges of life. This practice is just as varied as life itself, and there are almost as many kinds of practice as ways of life. This rubs off on the logic of practice. There is no logic for all variants of practice – rather each kind of practice has to create its own logic, its own modus operandi. However, there is one common trait characterizing the logic of all practices in contrast to the logic of all theorizing. There is no apriori, just aposteriori justification of practice. The conclusion of a practical inference is the very action or sequence of actions that we think makes it possible to realize our intentions under certain given circumstances. The rightness and rationality of our doing will thus only show up in the future, and we can never be sure of it in advance. This makes the logic of practice time-dependent and creative instead of a timeless justification or confirming way of reasoning. Theoretical logic looks backwards, practical logic looks forward.

   Logic is usually associated with theorizing, and practice is usually understood in contrast to theory. In my considerations below I will show that this theory-practice dichotomy is misleading and I will demonstrate why it makes sense to talk about a logic of practice.

The concept of practice

The philosophical term 'practice' is, according to Mittelstraß (1995), an expression for human life-activity in general, and is understood as interaction with environmental reality. In this sense the concept of practice has given reason to a lot of opposing and differentiating conceptualisations in the history of philosophy. Mittelstraß (1995) mentions exemplarily the concepts of labour, action, poiesis, and theory.

It seems clear that 'labour' and 'action' are samples for differentiation, while 'poiesis' and 'theory' could be samples of concepts related to 'practice' in an oppositional way. Talking about conceptualisation – fundamental for thinking activity in general and for philosophical work especially – there are at least two different ways to do it:

1. by characterising a phenomenon by comparing it with similar but specifically different phenomena: practice and labour for example or,
2. by illuminating a phenomenon by relating it to something in opposition to it: practice versus theory for example.

Note: anyway that doing labour and doing theory resembles practicing in human being activities. To explore which kind of logic asserts itself to the concept of practice I will adopt a concept-building method, which Nørreklit (2008) called "complementary ontological conceptualising". It is distinctive for this method that it focuses on conceptual complementarity in order to detect correlations in a larger conceptual field and to enable a holistic understanding of concepts. An analytical method of conceptualising would instead compare and differentiate a concept with similar concepts – affording this way classification and pule solving (see Nørreklit, 2008).

Complementary, holistic conceptualisation takes thus not only similar, but also opposite concepts as constituents of the meaning-environment of a particular concept. This way a concept is also meaningfully related to genuine alternatives of itself. Against this background, the traditional meaning-opposition between 'practice' and 'theory' makes clear that practice has to be understood within the meaning horizon of theory – and vice versa. The link between these opposites is – as I indicated above – the concept of acting. Thinking, we could say, is a non-practical activity but tinted by practice in the same way as practice is a non-theoretical activity tinted by theory. According to Kant (1912), practice is not every kind of manipulation, but only the bringing about of ends by observing general procedure rules (Kant, 1912, p. 175).

However, Kant (1912) believed that the opposition between theory and practice needed an intermediate to make theory practicable and practice reasonable. This intermediate consists of what he called the power of justification (Urteilskraft). It is this faculty of human thinking that is able to find out if a general principle can be applied to a case[1]. Insofar it resembles Aristotle's concept of phrónesis (Aristotle, 1991; Nussbaum, 2009). Theoretical knowledge without understanding its applicability to real cases, i.e. without Urteilskraft/phrónesis, is inefficient and so no *real* knowledge. At most it is a draft to a possible theory that still has to prove its applicability and thereby its practicability.

Of course the relation of theory and practice is not as simple as correspondence theories of meaning try to make it. There is no one-to-one correspondence between thinking and experiencing reality. There is no universe of things (res[2]) waiting for being caught by concepts – regardless of individual, type, attribute or relation concepts. We don't possess thinking schemes – as Kant still believed – which we just need to impose on what there is "outside" among a world of "things in themselves". In other words, concepts and things don't just correspond to each other – a priori thinking and a posteriori experiencing don't just match. There is always a lot of intermediating activity to do in order to approximate thinking, doing and experiencing. This intermediating activity is the epistemological function of what I understand by 'practice'.

Though this is just epistemological trial and error, I would like to say that 'practice' and 'theory' are not pure conceptual opposites but complementary opposites. It makes no real sense to talk about pure theory or pure reason on the one hand and pure reality (Kant's "Ding an sich") or pure practice handling it on the other. Let's keep hold of our train of thoughts hitherto that 'theory' and 'practice' as conceptual opposites at the same time are meaning-interwoven and so logically dependent on each other.

Interlude: what logic is about

Let's as a kind of interlude consider what logic is about. Modern logic is, according to a majority of 20th century and present logicians, about valid inferences. To investigate which kinds of conclusions you can infer from given premises, the modern logician constructs formal languages by determining a vocabulary of basic expression-types, a syntax for forming propositions, semantics to interpret propositions, and inference rules to determine valid arguments. Classical logic (see e.g. Kant, 1958) used to be subdivided into logic of concepts, logic of judgements, and logic of inferences. Both approaches, the classical and the modern, investigate – by analysing or constructing – forms of thought and how we, by forming thoughts, are able to pass from some preliminary knowledge into some new – or at least hitherto undetected/ unconscious - knowledge. Different forms of thought, i.e. different forms of concepts, propositions, and proposition connections, correspond to different forms of thinking activities: formation of concepts (conceptualising), of propositions (predication), and of propositional complexes (text, theory). The thinking transition from concepts to propositions, and from individual propositions to the totality of a theoretical or textual complexion of propositions that creates understanding and knowledge is in my optics what logic – from a philosophical point of view – is about.

In my considerations about the logic of practice, I copy the classical approach. I started, as you may have noticed, by looking at the conceptual circumstances characterising the conceptual field around 'practice'. After some investigation into the complementary – oppositional and differential – peculiarities of the concept of practice, there should follow an inquiry of the syntax or "propositional structure"[3] of practice. Which constituents of what we are prepared to call 'practice' have to be connected to make up a practice? Here it will become clear that practice is a higher order activity – an activity of activities. The concept of 'action' will be critical here to understand the logical structure of 'practice'. In short, 'practice' can be understood as a complex of spatiotemporal structured actions. Eventually we have to consider as an even higher order of practice complexions the field structure of practices, i.e. how practices form a complementary (opposition-difference) structure of higher order practices. This is what Bourdieu (1993) called 'practice field'.

Ending the interlude here I return to the interrupted main thread of conceptual considerations.

Continuing conceptualising - practice versus labour and versus poiesis

Let's next take a look at the difference between 'practice' and 'labour'. Again, both are human activities. The labour a person does will normally consist of a lot of different practices. Let's take the work of the owner of ecological groceries. She has for instance to combine the practice of driving a car or motorbike from her home to the office in one of her groceries – and home again after work; moreover the practice of doing office work: writing and reading e-mails, talking via telephone to suppliers, checking statistics about sold and stored products, talking to employees and customers; taking in and advertising new products or dropping established ones, when they don't sell any more, etc. She also has to do the bookkeeping or delegate it to one of her employees. Sometimes she experiences her work as laborious and wishes to be free from it. Then she dreams of having enough money not to be constrained any more to do her grocery labour. Thus labour, being a complex lot of different practices can be experienced as constraining and laborious, while some or all of the practices separately can be experienced unstrained and refreshing. Labour is a complexity of practices but not all practices are labour. People perform labour practices to earn money or other values that can be measured by (compared with) money.

Understood this way, labour equals what the Greeks called 'poiesis' – an action or a practice having its end outside itself. Nobody (but workaholics) works for work's sake. The Greeks, however, called actions or practices done for their own sake, 'praxis'[4]. You can dance just for the sake and pleasure of dancing; you can have a conversation with your friends just for the sake of amicable communication; you can think about the world and the meaning of your existence just for the sake of thinking and because you are a lover of wisdom – a philosopher. In any case, this was the way – according to Arendt (1958; 2008) – the classical Greek philosophers thought. Praxis, doing things for their own sake, is thus interrelated with the idea of freedom. That freedom also has its price is perhaps a much later insight. In the case of the Greeks this price was slavery. The polis-citizens could only be free from poietic activities - i.e. working for their sustenance - to the extent they owned slaves that performed those activities in their favour.

This critical comment notwithstanding, it is an interesting question if we, within the horizon of the whole of our life activities, are able to perform practices we are willing to do for their own sake. I think this connects the logic of practice to the logic of ethics. If human action and practice is bound to the realisation of (practical, aesthetic or epistemic) values, then ethics – in my opinion – is about the higher order value of our striving for the realisation of all these values[5].

Our modern expression 'practice' doesn't differentiate between doing something that has its end outside itself (poiesis) and doing things for their own sake (praxis). We can go for a walk with our dog just for the pleasure of walking, looking at the landscape around us, the cloud formations in the sky, smelling the soil and the wood, and giving the dog time to ramble around and sniff whatever he wants to sniff at. But we can also go for a walk in order to do something healthy for ourselves and the dog. Can we infer from this modern understanding of practice that in the final analysis we don't believe it possible to do something just for doing it – and not for reaching a particular end? - I am not sure.

I think a positive or negative answer is a question of ideology or – to use a more neutral expression – of mentality. By 'mentality' I will designate the way people think the world is and works and what it means for them to exist in it. Mentality is then the result of what we understand by 'human condition' (See Arendt 2008; 1958). To be human means being – not all the time but sometimes – conscious about existing in a real world as the wholeness of everything there is, happens, is done, and is experienced. To be conditioned in one's existence this way means – if we want it or not – to be constrained to search for and to bring about meaning in our life.

For this searching and bringing-about I adopt the concept of *activity*, and I don't want to differentiate between bodily, unconscious, unwilling, unintentional, and practical, conscious, willing and intentional activity. When I want to mark this difference I call the last variant, i.e. conscious etc. activity, *action*. Actions can be more or less simple or complex. I say the concept of action is *elastic* or *flexible* regarding simplicity/complexity. I don't think it makes sense to talk about absolutely simple or basic actions. I regard activity/action as the missing link in classical epistemology and philosophy of mind between being conscious and being simpliciter; or between, if you like, mind and matter, subject and object, and similar concept dualities.

To shift perspective a little, I want to highlight my conceptual considerations hitherto also from an information-theoretical angle. Understanding both physical and mental being as an informational process, I consider activity/action as a *medium* or (more dynamically expressed) *mediation* between being simpliciter and being conscious. – We experience, feel, and think that we are and what we are and in which kind of reality we are because and when we[6] are active.

The "connective" structure of action and practice

Let's go on and try to localise 'practice' within the horizon of the activity/action conceptual field[7]. Like 'action', the concept of 'practice' is elastic regarding simplicity/complexity. This is to say that 'action' and 'practice' don't differ because of their different complexity. Every practice consists of the performing of actions – more or less simple/complex ones. Driving a car is a practice that consists of a lot of more or less typical activities/actions that a person has to execute to succeed in driving a car. The conceptual difference between these activities/actions and the practice of car driving is that the latter is something a person performs not only once or twice, but usually several times. This aspect of *habit* makes 'practice' a forming or moulding factor of a practitioner's life (history).

As v. Wright (especially in v. Wright, 1967) made clear, actions create/produce histories of the actor(s) performing or participating in it. This holds a fortiori for practices. The way an actor or a collective of actors practices their life is essential for the kind of history they realise(s). Histories are then not only the result of single (though perhaps very complex) actions but of practices. This has also to do with the circumstance that practices normally are not limited to one (individual or collective) actor. Practices are usually society- and culture-relative action patterns or lifestyles.

Until now I have investigated the "propositional logic" of the concept of practice; i.e. how actions can be *connected* with other actions to constitute/bring about practices. It is a very interesting question which *practical connectives* there exist and how they exert their connecting force. It seems immediately clear that one of the factors that constitute the necessary internal coherence of actions making up a special practice must be temporal. It is for instance critical for the performance of cooking that the temporal order of doing things to prepare a special kind of dish is not completely optional. To boil potatoes you have to first put water and the potatoes in a pot and then heat the water on a cooking stove. Practices are thus time-sensitive.

Something similar holds for the spatial circumstances of practice performing. You can't perform any kind of practice everywhere you want. To perform a bicycle tour you need roads or at least something that has similar properties – a terrain supporting your (and your bicycle's) weight that is not too bumpy; you couldn't do it on a body of water, for instance. All kinds of practice that involve spatial movements of the practitioner presuppose that there is space to perform these movements – space to move different parts of his or her body, room to move from one spatial position to another; and there has to be a spatial connection between the different positions.

In other words, practices are both space and time sensitive. The same can be expressed by: practices are *situation* sensitive. In understanding the concept of 'situation' I refer to Barwise & Perry (1999). They define it as spatio-temporal located thing(s) having properties and relations.

Here, the critical meaning-aspect is the localisation of the entities "filling out" or constituting a situation. Their spatio-temporal localisation makes them *real* or *actual*[8].

Being situation-sensitive is decisive for the concept of practice because a practice-form or practice-type – like teaching philosophy, reading a novel, playing tennis – becomes only a practice when being *performed*. The performance of an action or a practice is, however, only possible in real/actual situations. It has to *take place* and *time* and has to be *done* by one or several *actors* using one or several *means* on one or several *objects* to *realise* one or several *intentions*.

Another expression for the situation-sensitiveness of the concept of practice is its *contingency*. A practice can only realise something – i.e. making it real or actual – by hic et nunc (accidentally) bringing it about and making it happen. Practicing something is then neither necessary nor just possible. If it were necessary it wouldn't be necessary to perform it. It would happen by itself[9]. We did not have to bother to do anything at all. If it was possible, but not interesting enough, that someone would make an effort to realise it, then it wouldn't really be a practice. In a way we could say a practice is only legitimated by its performance. We could do a lot of things that are possible to do, but we don't do them because it's meaningless or worthless for us to do them.

That these modality considerations about the concept of practice aren't just chimerical can be seen from research of ethical issues. We could do a lot of research – say to find practices to terrify people most effectively – that in the end is not desirable for anybody (not even for terrorists) to perform.

The habitual or customary meaning of the concept of practice suggests that practices have to be learned by education and through socialisation processes. To master a certain practice presupposes *knowledge* of how to do it. This knowledge is a result of our adaptation to the physical and social environment, of social upbringing, or explicit education. As a consequence, practices are usually socially approved action-patterns. According to v. Wright (1976) they are *institutionalised behaviour* (cf. V. Wright 1977, p. 135). A practice being institutionalised means "that it is performed by a community in which we grow into by learning to participate in this practice" (v. Wright 1976, p. 135).

The transition from doing things in a certain way to performing a social approved practice implies that doing things that way can become a custom or even a practical rule or norm. As a pattern of how to act in a particular situation – for instance how to behave when having dinner with friends – a practice represents not only the (historical) experience of a society but also its *culture* or system of values. Practices have thus to do with the historical process of transforming describable actions into prescriptive action patterns (schemes) or practices (See Brandom, 1994).

To sum up: practices are used to be socially institutionalised action-patterns that are learned by habituation, training or education. They consist normally in a complex of different but spatio-temporal connected actions. Comparing the logic of action and practice with propositional logic, the connection of actions to make up a practice corresponds to the conjunctive connective expressing that two or more propositions (at the same time) are true. Connecting actions *A* and *B* means simply to perform both *A* and *B* either at the same time and place, or in a temporal and spatial connection (succession, contiguity).

The internal structure of action and practice

Arriving at this point of my considerations, I think it is reasonable to go back one step. From investigating the structure (connectivity) of practices as complex actions let's jump into the very structure of action itself. What looks like the "predicate logic" of action or, in other words, what is the internal structure of an action?

I will start my search with the feature of actions I have already named above – marking the difference between propositions and actions. Actions, I said, not only represent but change the world. Apparently, the representational force of propositions lies in the relation between predicate and its argument(s). From an ontological point of view, this relation corresponds in one way or other to the complementarity of the substantial and the energetic appearance of real beings. To be real means both to happen (take place) and to be something (be a thing). From a logical point of view, predicates represent the energetic or event side, and predicate arguments[10] the substantial ("real", thing, object) side of a real being. It's nothing new but worth mentioning again, that in the history of modern logic it was Frege's (1891) flash of genius to interpret the relation between (logical) subject and predicate as a representational function between an object and the result of performing the operation, which the function represents, with this object. A proposition becomes thus the result or product of an operation that represents something by another thing. Representation is then no longer a passive mirroring or reflex of something by/on another (reflecting) thing. It is the (real) effect of an (acting) cause, i.e. the result of a change in the world.

If we take the concept of 'action' in its broadest English-speaking sense, namely representing the active or energetic part of (complementary) reality, then Frege's idea of understanding predicates as (representing) functions or operations mark a "logical turn" from onto-logical to ergo-logical[11] thinking.

The main difference between these two thinking-styles is the difference between re-presentation (sic!) and (re-)production. A physically and practically acting world produces reality – permanently conserving (reproducing) itself and changing. An ontologically or essentialistically understood world just represents reality – permanently repeating the same (essence) of things (substances). It isn't the place here to design the logic of practice as a fully developed language that satisfies the standards of modern formal logics. What I can do is, according to Segerberg (1992), to supply some philosophical work that "prepares the way for rigorous theorising" (Segerberg, 1992, p. 347). He continues: "Before the gold can be mined (the task of philosophical logic) prospectors must explore the terrain (the task of philosophy)" (Segerberg, 1992, p. 347).

Concluding remarks

Hopefully I have brought some distinctive traits of the logical terrain of the concept of practice to light, I will make some preliminary remarks here on the difference between the logic of representation and the logic of action. The former consists in proportion or relation of beings (entities). The predicate in a proposition represents the (conceptual) traits of a thing common with other things. The argument (logic subject) of the predicate identifies the thing (res) that is characterised by being related to other things with similar properties.

Before going on and trying to shed light on the logical peculiarities of action and practice, I have to call the reader's attention to an ambivalence that accompanies our understanding of logic. Since its Greek origins the term 'logic' has been understood as both the internal and connective *form* (structure and functioning mode) of phenomena, and the linguistic representation of this form. The same holds for predicative and – let me give the logic of action and practice a common name – pragmatic logic. The latter, i.e. the logic of action and practice, has – in order to understand it – to be represented by a language that corresponds to the real/actual logic of actions and practices. Obviously the linguistic representation of an action or a practice is not identical with the represented action or practice. The proposition 'Anna goes for a walk with her dog' is no walk for Anna with her dog. It is, however, an adequate or inadequate linguistic representation of what she and the dog are doing when going for a walk together.

I mention this ambivalence of what we mean by 'logic' in order to express my conviction that natural languages during their long history have developed more or less adequate means of expression for the most crucial structure- and function-elements of the logic of action and practice. Let me at least mention some.

The most distinctive difference between predicate and – as I called it above – pragmatic logic is that predication relates things to other things, which together represent a concept – i.e. a type of things or a property which makes things that have it comparable to each other. In contrast, actions and practices *cause situations* – i.e. states of affairs, events, processes. Causation by actions – practical causation – means that an agent voluntarily changes, preserves or prevents a situation. To be able to do this the agent has to be a conscious (sensing, feeling and thinking) being, either disposing of the necessary bodily conditions to perform the needed action themselves or possessing adequate communicative skills to make another agent perform the action.

The way in which some natural languages express these preconditions for acting is what in grammar is called *finite verb*. It is the personally and temporally flexed verb that represents the role of the agent and of the spatio-temporal (situational) contingency of actions. Actions have to be realised to be real/actual actions. Not realised but intended actions can in natural languages be expressed by *infinite verbs*. 'To read a book' is not a real/actual action but only a type or possibility to act in a certain way. To become an action it needs an agent that is able to read and does (performs) it at a particular point in time and at a particular place using a particular book as the object and also as the instrument or means of his reading. Thus, by person- and tempus-related flexion of the verb, some natural languages are able to represent the causing or generative form (structure/function) of pragmatic logic.

Another aspect of this logic is its societal character. Most or perhaps all actions and practices are not only learned by social interaction and communication but are – in the course of social histories – also *formed* and developed by a plurality of agents or collectives of agents. Natural languages express this circumstance again by finite verb flexion – here: singular/plural flexion. When you hear that 'John and Mary were eating dinner' there is an indication that they probably had dinner together.

My philosophical considerations of the logic of practice are at best preliminary and in any case very fragmentary. I tried to "explore the terrain" of the structure and functionality of pragmatic logic. In my opinion, the most significant fact I found – if I found something significant – is the difference between onto and ergo-logical forms of thinking. This implies that a developed logic of action and practice shall have to substitute the representing logic of predication by a causing/effecting logic of practice.

Notes

1. Kant says: "It is obvious that there has to be a connecting and transcending intermediate between theory and practice regardless how self-contained the theory may be; because the intellectual concept (Verstandesbegriff) that contains the rule has to be completed by an act of justification (Urteilskraft) whereby the practitioner decides if something is a case of the rule or not" (ibidem, my translation). Kant complements – and thereby forecasting Wittgenstein's "Philosophical Investigations" discussion to which degree our actions can be determined by rules – that it isn't possible to unlimitedly give rules to the justification of subsuming a case under a concept – "because this would go into infinity" (ibidem). This is a cardinal point in understanding the logic of practice – as Bourdieu 1993/1980 so emphatically has underlined.
2. The English expression 'reality' – originating from Latin 'res' and meaning something like 'world of things' – for the dynamic, changing world is misleading. The constituents of a changing world are complementary entities that only are things (substance) in as much they are also events (energy).
3. Of course, practices and their action constituents aren't propositions in the normal sense of the concept. Understood as the semantic content of a predication, a proposition *represents* a possible or actual situation, i.e. a state, event or action. The meaning of an action is in contrast not to represent but to change or conserve a situation. We talk here about the cardinal difference between *showing* (making recognisable) and *effecting* (producing, conserving, preventing) something.
4. The human life – understood as 'bios', i.e. something that can be described by a biography - is according to Aristotle (Politics 1254a7) a *praxis*. As a consequence, Aristotle must have thought life should be lived for its own sake.
5. I use practical, aesthetic, epistemic and ethical values as a basis for my standard classification of practice forms. We perform different kinds of practice to realise different kinds of valuable things, and thereby different kinds of meaning with our lives.

6 Note that I don't want either – in any way for the present – to disjoin bodily and mental existence and to say IT to the former and I to the latter. If I could be without being embodied in a bodily, physically real world I wouldn't bother to philosophise about all these questions.
7 By the way, I consider 'field' – inspired by Bourdieu 1993 – as a dynamical connection of physical, mental or practical forces resulting in an interrelation of (physical, mental, practical) entities bearing or performing these forces. Fields are thus *potentials* for physical, mental or practical actions.
8 It is an interesting trait of the English language that you have (at least) two different and in fact complementary possibilities to express that something happens or is part of the real world. 'Real' as mentioned above is derived from the Latin substantive 'res' in the sense of 'thing' or something *substantial*. 'Actual' is by contrast derived from the Latin verb 'agere' meaning to do or to effect, and alludes thus to the dynamic aspect of reality while 'real' alludes to its substantial aspect. The dynamical aspect is also accentuated by 'factual' – coming from Latin 'facere' meaning to do or to act.
9 According to v. Wright 1963 "to act is, in a sense, to *interfere* with 'the course of nature'" (ibidem, 36). Pörn 1977 has called this interferential feature of actions "counteractive conditionality". By his action an agent causes a change in the world that would not have taken place without his (or another agent's) action.
10 By the argument of a predicate what I mean here is in accordance with modern logic usage and what in classical logic and grammar has been called (logical, grammatical) subject.
11 I don't know if someone before me has made up a similar word. I derive it from the Greek verb 'érgein', 'doing', 'acting'. The 'onto' part in the term 'ontological' derives – as is well-known – from the Greek expression for 'being' 'on', which declines 'ontos', 'onti', 'onta' – in the masculine singular version. It is also related to the substantive 'ousia', which became translated to Latin both by 'substance' and 'essence'. The above mentioned turn from ontological to ergological thinking means thus a transition from substantial to energetic or from realistic to actionistic thinking. The mentioned Greek verb 'érgein' makes up the semantic stem of the substantive 'enérgeia' from which our modern term 'energy' originates. I name these etymologic relations to pave the way for my conviction that the logic of practice can be developed and explicated from the basis of a – lateral-thinking formulated – actio- or ergo-logical understood "ontology".

References

Arendt, Hannah, 2008 (1978). *Vita active.* München. Piper.

Aristoteles, 1991. *Nikomachische Ethik.* Zürich/München. dtv/Artemis Verlag.

Barwise, Jon & Perry, John, 1999. *Situations and Attitudes.* Stanford. CSLI Publications.

Bourdieu, Pierre, 1993 (1980). *Sozialer Sinn.* Frankfurt am Main. Suhrkamp.

Brandom, Robert B., 1994. *Making It Explicit.* Cambridge, Massachusetts. Harvard University Press.

Kant, Immanuel, 1912. Über den Gemeinspruch: Das mag in der Theorie richtig sein, taugt aber nicht in der Praxis, in: Kant, I., 1912. *Vermischte Schriften,* Leipig. Insel Verlag, 175-220.

Mittelstraß, Jürgen, 1995. *Enyklopädie Philosophie und Wissenschaftstheorie.* Bd. 3, Stuttgart/Weimar. Verlag J.B. Metler.

Nørreklit, Lennart, 2008. *Kritisk ontologisk konceptualisering.* Aalborg. unpublished.

Nussbaum, Martha, 2009. *The Fragility of Goodness.* Cambridge: Cambridge University Press.

Pörn, Ingmar, 1970. *The Logic of Power.* Oxford. Basil Blackwell.

Pörn, Ingmar, 1977. *Action Theory and Social Science.* Dordrecht. D. Reidel Publishing Company.

Segerberg, Krister, 1992. *Getting Started: Beginnings in the Logic of Action,* in: *Studia Logica 51.* p. 347-378.

Wright, Georg Henrik von, 1967. *The Logic of Action – A Sketch,* in: Rescher, N. (ed.), 1967. *The Logic of Decision and Action.* University of Pittsburgh Press, p. 121-139.

Wright, G. H. v., 1976. *Determinism and the Study of Man,* in: Manninen, Juha. and Tuomela, R. (eds.), 1976. *Essays on Explanation and Understanding. Studies in the Formation of Humanities and Social Sciences.* Dordrecht. D. Reidel Publishing Company, p. 415-435. German translation in: v. Wright, G. H., 1977. *Handlung, Norm und Intention, Untersuchungen ur deontischen Logik.* Berlin, New York. Walter de Gruyter, p. 131-152.

Lars Bo Henriksen

Praxis, PBL and the application of knowledge

> "Alles rechte Verstehen ist Anwendung"
> "All true understanding is application"
> *Gadamer*

Introduction

It is a general notion that there is an inherent conflict between theory and practice. "The education is too academic, too theoretical", - one regularly hears - "The candidates are theoretically strong, but their knowledge is of little relevance to the labour market". This notion points to a general problem in any educational endeavour: how to transform classroom activities into useful knowledge, knowledge that is relevant to the student's future trade or profession. PBL (problem based learning) may be viewed as one attempt to bridge and somehow overcome this theory-practice dilemma. Students in a PBL environment work on as close to real-life-problems as possible. The general philosophy of PBL, and its ability to create knowledge that is relevant for the student's future trade or profession, can be extended further by taking the learning process into the real-life environment. This is what is known as internship, or "praktik" in Danish and German.

In this chapter, the learning process associated with internship "praktik" is the primary focus. What processes take place and what kind of learning takes place, when students from a PBL learning environment engage themselves in an internship – praktik - arrangement? The learning experience is obviously different from that of the ordinary classroom, but what form will the learning take? Will the students learn as much as in the classroom or will they learn something differently? And just as importantly, how can we understand and describe the learning processes when we have to take this world outside the classroom into consideration.

The structure of the remainder of the chapter is as follows. First, I will present a case of an engineering student spending a five month internship in an engineering company, working on different assignments together with fully qualified engineers. This leads to a discussion of the kind of knowledge gained during the internship/praktik. It is obviously different from what the student could have learned by staying in the classroom, but in what respect is it different? In this discussion the hermeneutic concept of application or "anwendung" plays a central role.

The praktik
Bachelor integrated praktik

> Bachelor training includes an individual praktik (praktikum, internship). The purpose of the praktik is that students gain practical experience in addition to the teaching on campus. The practical arrangements concerning the praktik is organised in a way that students during the 6th and/or 7th semester are in a praktik continuously for approximately half a year, in all 30 ECTS[1]. The Study Board shall appoint a praktik coordinator among the teachers.
> (From the study programme, Bachelor in Engineering, Aalborg University)

At Aalborg University the study programmes (studieordning) were recently modified, so that they would comply with other study programmes at Danish technical colleges. All bachelor programmes in engineering at the technical colleges have always included an element of internship (praktik). At Aalborg University the previous study programmes did not include internship as engineering education was allowed an exception from internship due to the PBL-structure and nature of its pedagogy. It was previously argued that Aalborg engineering students would gain sufficient practical experience from the project- and group-work, which formed the central part of their studies. From 2007 this was changed, and internship was made compulsory for Aalborg University's engineering students. This change was not made on the basis of pedagogical arguments (e.g. - the students would learn more from the internship which will enhance the overall quality of the engineering education received), but may be viewed as a classic budget cutting exercise. The Ministry of Education does not have to pay the university any fees for the five to six months of internship.

We draw in this chapter on the experiences of Karl, who was among the first students from Aalborg University to participate in the new internship programme. With the new study programmes, the fifth semester (first half of the third year) is dedicated to the internship. The semester is structured as follows: (i) students are offered training courses equal to 12 ECTS. These courses are held at the beginning of the semester, from February until the end of March. The internship, equal to 18 ECTS, then begins in early April and lasts until September or October, with the possibility of a short summer break. Karl's internship was prepared through a training course, especially targeted at the problems and challenges foreseeable in the internship and courses of a more engineering specific content. The intervening period from January through March was also used to initiate several contacts with the internship sponsoring company. The university supervisor provided the initial contact to the company. Through these contacts it was agreed that Karl would work in the engineering department and that he would work on a very specific project in motor regulation. Before arriving at the company in early April, Karl had participated in training courses in motor regulation theory; so, one would expect him to be very well qualified and prepared for the task on motor regulation.

The definition of the student's tasks was based on the company's urgent need to solve a very specific problem related to motor regulation in one of their machines. These machines were already in production, but not working satisfactorily. During this internship (praktik) Karl worked closely with a group of engineers, especially his contact person "Anton". The project task was to produce a model of the motor, a model of its regulation, and to optimise the relevant software. Through several tests it was concluded that the motor would start and run better with the new software and consequently the new software was implemented in all new machines and was stored for implementation in future machines. Real engineering work was done and real engineering problems were solved.

The internship was documented in a report (66 pages and appendices) and the report and the internship were evaluated at an oral examination, lasting about two hours, with an external examiner from industry and a supervisor from the university. Karl was very pleased with the internship; he learned a lot and he found out what it was like to work in an engineering environment and to work on solving real engineering problems in a workplace situation.

> "I had to take care of everything in the assignment – from software to hardware, everything" (Karl)

Equally important, according to Karl, were interaction, communication and cooperation with the other engineers on site, who were very willing to help, whenever help was needed. The ability to solve the assignment problem and the ability work on an equal footing with fellow engineers provided a significant boost to the self-esteem of this engineer-to-be and to his sense of identity as a budding member of the engineering profession.

The supervisor from the University was also fully in agreement that the internship had been of great value to students, including Karl. But she had some reservations. First, she was able to reach the same conclusions as the students; confidence and the boosting of self-esteem is a good thing. But she found something missing. Normally, in a PBL programme at Aalborg University, students work in a group on a specific project assignment. They would also help, or rather educate, one another with the problems presented to them in the training courses. This peer learning is missing in the praktik and the students consequently miss that part of their education. The result is, perhaps, a less secure handling of theoretical issues presented in the training courses and a less secure handling of theoretical problems not present in the internship assignment. This also points to a possible weakness related to the training courses as they are not an integrated part of the internship semester, but are the same courses designed for those students who continue their studies to master degree level[2]. Therefore, the internship students will not get the same qualifications from the courses as the master's students, benefitting from the peer learning in the groups. So, even if the internship provides a very positive experience, as Karl's evidence attests, there are some possible weaknesses in the way the entire fifth semester is organised – the very tight schedule of the training courses in February and March makes it difficult for the internship students to benefit from peer learning and thereby reach a level normally expected in the Aalborg tradition. This is suggestive of some possible changes in the overall programme, but again the pedagogical arguments would fall short compared to the missing economy in the whole internship programme.

This all raises some important questions. First, what and how did Karl learn during his internship? As noted above, he was certainly very pleased with the experience and he said that he learned a lot. Conversely, his supervisor from the university was not all that impressed; she maintains that he could have learned more by staying at the university. To address this divergence, we need to know what Karl really did during his internship. However, to explore and make some sense of this difference of opinion on "learning" between Karl and his supervisor we need to know what it means to have learned something. In the following sections I first confront the key question - what does it mean to learn something? Secondly, I will look at Karl's experiences during his internship – what did he really do during this internship?

Teacher centred education and internship
The word praxis is Greek and holds several meanings depending on both context and the conceptualisation of the word itself. According to Aristotle praxis is "the actions of free men" and is one of three actions that free men can perform – the others being theoria and poesia. Praxis then consists of economia, ethics and politics. Praxis can be good 'eupraxis' or bad 'dyspraxis'. Finally, praxis is another name for Aphrodite – goddess of love and beauty! We see here that the word praxis is an ancient word with several possible meanings. As Wittgenstein reminds us – the meaning of a word is how it is used.

In present day usage and debate, praxis is often contrasted with theory, as we noted in the example above - "Education is too theoretical" it was said. Thereby, a dichotomy between theory and practice is established which, from an educational point of view, is rather unfortunate as in any education, especially engineering education, the one cannot do without the other. We can now point to the old adage, often attributed to Kant that "Theory without practice is void and practice without theory is blind". It follows that theory/practice is a false dichotomy, and the division between theory and practice an artificial one. This false dichotomy regularly surfaces, however, when practice is used as a pedagogical device; that is, when practice is used to test theory that has been taught in the classroom.

Praxis as a pedagogical device is nothing new; Dewey, Freire, Lave and Wenger, Kolb and others have stressed the importance of combining classroom teaching with some kind of praxis, internship or doing/acting in general. These protagonists of 'praxis as pedagogical device' are often, rightly, attacking traditional classroom teaching for its shortcomings and promoting praxis as a better alternative or as a necessary complement. It is not the intention in this paper to rehash the voluminous pedagogical debates on this issue. It suffices for our purposes simply to state that this debate could start with a pragmatic understanding of education; we have learned something when we are able to appropriately apply what is learned in certain situations. In this case, Karl has learned about motor regulation theory when he is able to apply it to the motors in question in the internship company. This sounds fair enough, an engineer should of course be able to apply what is learned to engineering practice. But even if it sounds fair enough, it is not without its problems.

If learning is all about application it could be rather instrumentalist in the sense that what is learned is only learned in order to be applied. That could be learning to do without a proper understanding of what lies behind the doing, a kind of training of "a skill to the job" kind of learning reminiscent of the early days of Taylorism of de-skilling in early mass production. Such an approach to learning neglects other aspects such as *bildung*, tradition and deep understanding. Application is certainly important but the question is now raised of how application should find its place in the debate on learning and internship.

The problem of "having learned something" is often addressed where traditional teacher-centred teaching is under fire, what Freire refers to as the "banking model" (Freire 1970 cap 2). In the banking model of education we reduce what is learned to a reproduction of what the teacher said or what is written in text books. If we do that – reduce it to mere reproduction – then new knowledge would have a most difficult pathway into the world and there would be no reason for any internship whatsoever, as the teacher and the text book would be deemed to know it all. In the banking model we reduce education to schooling, and we reduce teaching to a question of optimal transfer of the explicit knowledge possessed by the teacher - a mere technical problem.

The banking model of education fits neatly into a narrow early modernist conception of education (Gallagher 1992 p. 169). Modernity here refers to the idea or set of ideas that can be understood as a special version of occidental thinking, dominant in the early Enlightenment. This form of thought is characterised by its rationalism (mainly of the instrumental variety), anti-traditionalism and scientism (Schanz 1990). Traditions are deemed to hold no value, as they are laden with superstition and should be avoided as a source of knowledge. Rather, science is seen as a reliable source that can provide true, valid knowledge. Rationality then tells us that there is one guiding logic that can show us the one best way, in economic or technological matters for example. Following this logic we should be able to emancipate ourselves from tradition, religion and the forces of nature and we should be able to live the good life guided by scientific knowledge and rationality. This narrow and overly instrumental focus is of course not without its problems, particularly in transferring the natural science model to the social sciences and its so called value-free nature, as it has become a tradition in itself. It is now highly contested in many fields, yet remains surprisingly tenacious in its hold on many.

There are other logics and science and scientific knowledge are not without their flaws. It is doubtful if these overly narrow and simplistic ideas alone could lead to living the good life considering their inherent flaws. Yet such ideas fit neatly into modern ideas of education and teaching where the teacher-centred model, for whatever reason, is the preferred option. In the teacher centred model, the role of the teacher is simply to transfer scientific knowledge to students. Students listen to their teachers and read textbooks and should thereby get access to true knowledge. The problem with this model in relation to internship is of course how the student should apply the knowledge gained in this way in the real world. The teacher centred model would in most cases imply some assignments, problems or other tasks that should prepare the students to apply such knowledge. The crux is that teaching and learning never leave the classroom and the application of such knowledge to real problems in the real world is never put to the test.

Yet another modern myth is the simplistic notion that technology is the application of scientific knowledge. In the case of praktik, the internship could then be seen as the application of the (scientific) knowledge transferred from teacher and banked by student. The key point being that the teacher's knowledge is the right knowledge and praktik is simply a matter of mere application. Neither the banking model nor this view of technology are accepted here – they are inherently flawed and an alternative conceptualisation is required if we are to gain a more substantive understanding of praktik and internship. The paper now moves to a discussion of the hermeneutic alternative.

The hermeneutic alternative
Hermeneutics offers an alternative to the teacher centred model (Gallagher 1992) as well as a critique of modernist thought in general (Gadamer 1960). Hermeneutics is concerned with the problem of understanding – what does it mean to understand something? This brings us

back to the question raised earlier in this chapter - what and how did Karl learn during his Internship? Any learning or understanding builds upon some previous knowledge. Our language in particular, but also all our prior experiences and what we have gained from our upbringing. Gallagher (1992) offers a model of learning building on hermeneutic principles. This understanding of learning includes the elements tradition, self-transition and production. These concepts and their relation to Karl's internship will now be addressed and explained in the following sections.

Tradition

"Understanding is to be thought of less as a subjective act than as participating in an event of tradition, a process of transmission in which past and present is constantly mediated" (Gadamer 1962 p. 277).

The knowledge that is a precondition for any learning Gadamer terms "prejudices". This is to be thought of as pre-knowledge and certainly not to be confused with its meaning in our daily use of language where prejudice has several negative connotations. Prejudices are not subjective in the sense that they are our private constructs; they will always be part of a horizon of meaning within which the knowledge, that is to be learned, makes sense. The horizon, that the prejudice is established within, is part of a tradition. Not tradition as in our ordinary language, where tradition is often viewed as representing something old, perhaps authoritarian or superstitious but certainly something that by any means should be avoided. Just as in the anti-traditionalism of modernity, for example. But in order to establish an understanding of texts, of social phenomena or of understanding itself, it is necessary to rehabilitate the tradition (Gadamer, 1960, p. 277).

The German word "Überlieferung" is actually better than the English translation "tradition". Überlieferung means that something is handed over or passed on from one generation to the next. Tradition represents knowledge and an authority that is able to help us understand, by acting as the prejudices that are a prerequisite for any understanding. In this sense engineering is a tradition and engineering students are introduced to this tradition through education. Tradition represents knowledge – e.g. engineering knowledge - and is affiliated to the authority of knowledge in a particular field - without necessarily acting authoritarian. Authority here is to be viewed in a positive sense. The tradition is a possibility for the engineer to know what it takes to *be* an engineer - through dialogue with tradition, it will be possible to develop the tradition and the knowledge that it represents. In this sense tradition is essential and the process through which future engineers, such as Karl, acquire this knowledge is known as *Bildung*. Bildung is the German word for education and is every bit as untranslatable as *Überlieferung*. Bildung signifies the process and the result of the process of education and Karl will be "Gebildet", when he has finished his education (Henriksen 2006).

Self-transcendence

Horizon is the individual starting point, but fortunately we are able to let our horizons meet other horizons. Thereby we are able to understand each other, understand texts, understand traditions and thereby learn something. Through a description of other horizons, both understanding and learning become possible. This allows understanding and learning to be described as a fusion of horizons.

The teacher centred model is also a tradition that seeks to teach the content of traditions, but in most cases in a way where only the teacher, and not the students, is active. The important thing here is, however, is students' active participation in the fusion of horizons and in the event of tradition. That is, the student should actively acquire the knowledge that is the tradition; and this cannot be transferred to a passive student. It is also important because traditions, in order to be kept alive, should be challenged and questioned by those who participate in the tradition. Only in this way can the tradition renew itself and be able to hand over or pass on (Überlieferung) meaningful knowledge. Active participation is therefore essential when one adopts a hermeneutic slant on education. Through the fusion of horizons and by active participation in the event of tradition the student transcends his own self – and he or she is changed in the process. One's horizon is broadened and one gradually over time and active participation acquires the knowledge of a tradition and thereby one is able to not only question one's own prejudices but change them as well.

Production

Being changed, being part of a tradition and having expanded one's horizons is to have learned something. But to have fully understood the knowledge of the tradition, the knowledge has to be applied, or to be able to apply is to have fully understood and thereby learned. But the knowledge of the tradition is a general knowledge and that general knowledge has to be applied to a specific situation. Karl's knowledge of motor regulation gained through his studies at the university had to be applied to a specific motor in a specific company in a specific situation. When he was able to do that, and he has deomonstrated that he did, then we can say that he has learned something. As Gadamer put it - Alles rechte Verstehen ist Anwendung – 'all true understanding is application' (Gadamer 1992). What Karl did, applying general knowledge to the specific situation, also points to the fact that a new situation requires the production of new knowledge. Therefore, being an engineer, and thereby being able to apply knowledge to new and specific situations is to be able to produce new knowledge specially suited to the situation and to the specific problem. Production then is not necessarily the production of a physical product, but of the production of new knowledge. This is to have learned something: to be able to produce new knowledge linked to a specific situation on the basis of a tradition.

Gadamer's analysis of phronesis - Ethics and judgement of a situation

In *Truth and Method* Gadamer (1992) confronts the problem of how to apply general knowledge to a specific situation. In Gadamer's analysis of understanding this is shown through an analysis of Aristotle's concept of phronesis (Gadamer 1960, pp. 312). Phronesis is for Aristotle one of three types of knowledge each of which describes various aspects of human life. The three ways of knowing are phronesis, techne and episteme.

Episteme describes a form of knowledge which is universal and independent of time and space. The classic example is mathematics. Episteme could also refer to the knowledge of the natural sciences, seeking universal laws of nature. Techne is knowledge of arts and crafts. This is the knowledge of what products one wants to produce and also the ability to produce them. This knowledge is dependent on the situation and the people and things, objects or artifacts involved in the production. Phronesis is a social and ethical knowledge that is needed in order for people to be able to commit themselves to other people, to get on with other people, and to succeed and function appropriately in a social context.

As we noted above, the interpretation of tradition forms a central part in the process of understanding and learning. The question is then, how can we apply universal principles to a specific situation and thereby produce the knowledge necessary. This problem is the same as when we want to apply general ethical principles - phronesis: How can we apply universal moral principles to a particular situation. Through an analysis of the concept of phronesis Gadamer seeks to apply the same principles to the interpretation of tradition, because both phronesis and understanding address the problem of relating the universal (principles) to the particular (the situation).

Gadamer begins his analysis of phronesis by asking whether there is a particular philosophical understanding of morality, (the moral being of man) and the role of knowledge for moral issues (Gadamer 1962 p. 313). For Aristotle moral knowledge is of a different nature than, for example, knowledge of physics. Physics is governed by natural laws, but ethics can be described as instructions and rules and is therefore subject to change and influence through history and over time. The question now is whether phronesis is similar to techne or whether it resembles episteme. Phronesis can not be epistemic knowledge, as phronesis is not knowledge of an object. A situation where a person wants to find out what is the right thing to do is not objective. Situation and person are not independent, since such a situation requires knowledge (phronesis), action and commitment. Therefore, phronesis cannot be epistemic, because this kind of knowledge involves application; universal knowledge, for example mathematics, cannot guide people in a dynamically changing world.

"What Gadamer suggests through Aristotle, by contrast is that history is productive of real knowledge that is applicable because it differs and that it differs because it is applied. (Weinsheimer, 1985) ".

Therefore, phronesis is more like techne than episteme, since both techne and phronesis are applied knowledge. Both are similar to the kind of knowledge a craftsman uses to produce a given product. He has a general idea of what he wants to do, maintain, fix or make, what purpose it will serve, who will make use of it, and so on. Besides this general knowledge, he has a practical knowledge of materials, tools, processes and so on. All this knowledge was handed to him through tradition, through experience and through formal training as an apprentice. This is another form of learning because it is different from the teachings of the linear model and is specifically directed towards application. It is taught by someone who already possesses this knowledge, a master, and is a knowledge, which can be used immediately. Phronesis knowledge resembles this kind of craft knowledge.

In a situation where ethical knowledge is required a person has a general idea of what is right and wrong and this is acquired through bildung, through tradition. It is learned at an early age, before common sense can guide the child's actions, and it allows the general idea to serve as a prejudice; ethical knowledge cannot exist without prejudices. This general idea of knowing the right is insufficient as it also requires action and engagement in any particular situation, and when situations change it is not enough to determine what should be done in advance because the right thing to do is codetermined by the situation and demands judgement.

From this discussion we see that there are similarities between phronesis and techne; there are, however, also some differences. Man is not a material that can be changed similar to whatever material the craftsman works on. Craftsmanship can be learned and forgotten again, but not ethical knowledge. When right and wrong are learned, they are not forgotten. Techne can be described as a means to an end, but phronesis is much more than the means to achieve a goal. Phronesis is also about friendship, forgiveness, sense of community, and much more which is intensely social and human.

Gadamer concludes that his analysis of phronesis can serve as a model for hermeneutic understanding. This hermeneutic understanding refers not only to addressing the question of the tension between the general and specific; it is also a matter of application (Anwendung, anvendelse). Just as with phronesis, understanding is neither something that happens occasionally or by coincidence, but understanding and learning are from the very start a much more comprehensive and complex process – one based on tradition, prejudices and active participation of the actors involved.

Hermeneutics and praxis

From the discussion thus far on Gadamer's hermeneutics we can see that the internship Karl experienced is very similar to the learning process or form of knowledge that Gadamer and Aristotle refer to as techne. Acquiring techne demands some form of apprenticeship wherein the apprentice becomes acquainted with the traditions of the craft in question. Learning a craft produces useful and applicable knowledge. It is about being able to analyse a specific problem situation and then find the right tools, remedies and knowledge to address and solve such problems. But it is even more than that, because there is more than techne to the learning of craftsmen and engineers. This learning also involved knowledge of right and wrong within the tradition in question. Being "Gebilded" is about knowing the do's and don'ts of the trade – it is about ethics. Further it is also about phronesis, that is, how to be an engineer, how to behave as an engineer, and how to enact and learn to live one's identity as an engineer.

Comparing all this to the linear model demonstrates in no uncertain terms that when it comes to the learning processes of internship, hermeneutics offers us a much more comprehensive body of knowledge with which to address the learning processes involved. If internship only involved applying epistemic classroom and textbook knowledge, then there would be no reason for including an internship component in any bachelor of engineering programme. Why bother with all the hassle if the classroom model suffices? But as we can see from Gadamer's analysis, applying knowledge is a much more complex and interesting process. If we want to be able to more adequately understand what internship is and how students learn and do within such internships then we also need to consider phronesis, bildung, tradition and students' abilities to analyse a situation and produce relevant knowledge. This brings us back to Karl's experiences.

An engineering student in the real world

With the hermeneutic description of knowledge we can now turn to the question I raised above about the learning gained by Karl during his internship. It should by now, with hermeneutics in mind, be rather obvious that the linear model of learning is insufficient when trying to understand what internship is, the processes involved and its outcomes. An extreme interpretation of the linear model might look something like this; the school, college or university provides lessons presenting epistemic knowledge to the students. It is then up to students to find ways of applying this epistemic knowledge to real life problems and situations. With the description of techne above in mind it is plain to see that this would be quite unfortunate for any engineer-to-be. Engineering has many similarities to techne, as described above, and the training of engineers should of course reflect this.

With the tools and ideas of hermeneutics we are now much better positioned and try to analyse Karl's experiences during his internship and to find more plausible answers to our initial question; what and how did Karl learn during his internship?

During his internship Karl wrote in his diary about his work at the internship company. First day at the company was the 29th of April:

> "I turned in at eight thirty, I was shown a work place. Nine o'clock there was a meeting where I was welcomed and the oth-

ers asked what I was doing and so on. After the meeting I was
handed a PhD dissertation about "Advanced control methods
for optimisation of arc welding".

During these first days Karl is getting into the tradition and is improving and expanding on his prejudices. The following days Karl is settling in, getting an internet connection and so on, and reading up on the dissertation. Monday 5th May he writes:

"I was shown my place in the laboratory and 'Anton' showed
me how to conduct measurements on the welding process and
further reading in the dissertation".

Here Karl is handed over knowledge (techne in this case) by someone who knows (Anton - a master). From May 7th through May 14th he writes every day with very technical descriptions of his work on the measurements, the tests and the modelling. On May 14th he introduces a new assignment or group he is referring to when he writes:

"Meetings: Boost group. Wants to find a connection between
slow motion movie and the measurements".

When attending meetings and in discussions, phronesis is of course important, but he already knew that from the PBL-group work at the university. From May until the summer vacation in mid July, Karl only writes about technical matters in his diary, only briefly mentioning a meeting with his supervisors from the university on the 4th of July. After the summer holidays this continues, so the diary becomes more and more technical and more meetings, such as a supervisor meeting on August 14th and a general information meeting at the company on August 26th are again only briefly mentioned.

The technical side of the diary starts out with a short and very broad description of the assignment as something about a motor regulation in a welding machine and gradually, through working on and with the assignment, Karl becomes more familiar with the problem, which becomes more and more complicated. He starts out reading the PhD dissertation and after some days – the 5th of May - he starts working in the lab with some measurements on the welding process. On the 7th of May he performs some measurements on filters and he redesigns the filter 40KHz to 20 KHz, which solves some of the problems. On the 8th of May the measurements are used in a Mat-lab calculation programme and in a simulation programme. On May 19th he writes:

> "Meetings with the boost group. Motor regulation group. Print-line (A partnering company) (company visit). Analysis of motor regulation, and calculation of gears in relation to the speed of the welding wire. A Mat-lab file is made for storage and future use. The file is used for calculation of motor rotation in relation to the speed of the wire. Besides it can show the number of pulses.

20th of May he writes:

> "The existing motor steering is analysed, I have access to the key code to the Sigma machine (the machine carrying the wire in the welding machine) and I have found the control loop and made an (mathematical) expression for the regulator. It can be seen from the transfer function that it is a PI regulator. This is modelled in a simulation programme".

And on the 21st of May:

> "I can now code and compile new software for the Sigma machine (the one causing the problems). Spent most of the day debugging and the error is located to measurements in the microprocessor ." And later "When the model of the motor is completed it shall maybe be used as a basis for a Kahlmann filter ... in cooperation with Anton".

Karl continues his diary in this manner as yet more elements are drawn into the project as he gradually works his way towards solutions to the initial problem - the motor regulation. Through this he demonstrates how he is actually producing new knowledge. On the 3rd of June he writes:

> "Meeting with Anton on the status of my project and on which ways to go. I got a solution working at 50A. That is a solution that is concerned with the voltage – if it is above or beyond 20V. This solution is tested at 200A, where it did not work".

The diary has no final conclusion on the technical part, but it seems that a lot of tests, simulations and discussions made it possible to detect and locate the problem and, most impressively, made it possible to solve it. The actual solution was implemented, though, after Karl had left the company. Karl writes as a kind of conclusion to his report:

> "During my internship I have worked with a lot of assignments (topics) from pure hardware to regulation of systems. Through this process the focus has been on learning. This is seen in the boost converter project to the Company's welding machine – here I also got a lot of help from other engineers at the Company. We have also had visits from the AC company, supplier of capacitors – they have great knowledge of heat transfer from capacitors.
>
> Through the internship in this company, I have learned that working as an engineer is not entirely based on knowledge. It is also very much about coping with the other employees. Though you are working individually on specific problems, but if you get stuck, and can't get any further, it is nice to be able to talk to someone else and listen to [their] approach to the problem.
>
> Now, of course, this should not sound like I always ask for help. Because through the internship I have also learned how to get access to the newest knowledge within a new development. This, I think, I did not have before".

Considering Karl's experiences here, and based on the accumulated evidence, it is obvious this was not a linear process, and not simply a question of applying epistemic knowledge learned trough training courses. Epistemic knowledge of course plays a vital role for engineers, as when Karl used a mathematical model and a Mat-lab tool to model the motor regulation device. He also attended exams at the university twice during the internship. According to his diary he learned a lot and he learned that engineering is also about collective application and co-operation with colleagues. In the language of hermeneutics we could say that episteme, phronesis and techne are all central to substantive learning and Karl experienced these key insights this through the internship in a real work setting.

Internship is a process and can be understood as a learning process, producing new knowledge, solving problems and simultaneously changing/developing the student and his prejudices in the process. This is what Karl demonstrates unequivocally in his diary. He starts out by reading about welding processes in a PhD thesis. This is one way to become acquainted with the tradition. The process also involved the establishment of a problem statement, measurements, data, calculations, models etc. These are all activities which form part of an engineer's everyday life and when Karl was introduced to them he was also introduced to engineering as a tradition - and all this could only happen with the student's active participation in the process.

According to Karl it was interesting to participate, and still according to him, it was easy for him to get used to the work in the company as it in many respects resembled what he had been used to from the PBL environment at the university. Nothing new, business as usual as one can also argue that the Aalborg PBL environment incorporates episteme, techne and phronesis. Therefore, we can conclude that Karl learned to analyse a problem, produce new knowledge on the basis of a tradition and apply this new knowledge to new problems – he learned how to apply the general to the specific. He also learned to work as an engineer and work together with other engineers and, finally, he was "gebilded" and therefore able to identify himself as an engineer. With the aid of hermeneutics we are able to construct a much more comprehensive understanding of praxis learning and internship.

There is one question, though, that remains to be answered. Karl was very pleased with the internship, but his supervisor said that he could have learned more if he had stayed at the university, benefitting from the peer learning in the PBL-project group. From Karl's point of view the success of the internship was due to the success of his work on the assignment. He was able to solve the problems and he was able to act as a fully qualified engineer. The supervisor's reservations related to the theoretical knowledge behind the assignment. If Karl, she said, had stayed at the university he would have been able to fully understand what he was doing. What he did in the internship was fine, but he was not fully capable of handling all the math behind his solutions.

This disagreement could call for two different interpretations. First, Karl could say that application is more important than textbook knowledge, and he knew just enough of the theory to solve the problem and that is fine. He wants to be an engineer and not a mathematician. The supervisor, on the other hand, could say that she was worried that the knowledge he had would someday would prove insufficient, as the knowledge he had gained though university training and through the internship was the kind of training-to-the-job knowledge that I cautioned about earlier in this paper. She could maintain that the assignment was a success, yes, but only with a lot of help from others. Where the truth in this lies is difficult to judge, but again, it shows the complexity of the problem. Is Karl just trained to the job and would he hold only little understanding of the deeper theoretical insights of the field, or is the supervisor too concerned with reproduction of the epistemic classroom teaching? Both are up for debate.

Conclusions

I started out this chapter by asking what did Karl learn during his internship, how did he learn, and how could we conceptualise this learning. For obvious reasons briefly stated above the linear model is summarily rejected here. It offers no idea of application and reduces learning to mere schooling in epistemic knowledge. The hermeneutic alternative is much more comprehensive and is precisely about application. It also introduces the very useful concepts of phronesis, techne and episteme, providing us with much richer and deeper conceptualisations of the learning process. Through this we can see learning as a process where students actively participate, and need to participate, in the learning process. Learning then becomes a question of application which demands knowledge, engagement and action; and in Karl's case we observe the production or creation of new knowledge and its application to a certain problem in a specific situation within the context of an internship. Karl was introduced to engineering as a tradition, as an activity, as something that requires knowledge, engagement and action: this was what and how he learned.

As a general insight into engineering education there are certainly lessons to be learned here. If the hermeneutic alternative is able to show us anything, it is that learning a trade or profession such as engineering requires epistemic and technical knowledge as well as phronesis, and further, that active participation in the learning processes is necessary. Whether this learning takes place in a company as internship or in a PBL environment at the university, or both as in this case, can be a matter for further debate. What I have attempted to do here is to argue the case for adopting insights from hermeneutics in addressing such issues as these insights provide a deeper, richer and much more comprehensive understanding of the learning processes involved. "All true understanding is application"

Notes
1. European Credit Transfer and Accumulation System
2. The students who do not want to become bachelors, but wish to become masters, do not presently participate in the internship programme, and have their own PBL-based programme for the fifth semester.

References

Christensen, Jens; Henriksen, Lars Bo; Kolmos, Anette, 2006. *Engineering science, skills, and Bildung*. Aalborg. Aalborg University Press.

Dewey, John, 1997. *Experience and Education*. Pocket Books. Reprint edition.

Freire, Paulo, 1970. *Pedagogy of the oppressed*. New York. Continuum.

Gadamer, Hans-Georg, 1962. *Truth and Method*. New York. Crossroad.

Gallagher, Shaun, 1992. *Hermeneutics and Education*. Albany. State University of New York Press.

Henriksen, Lars Bo, 2006. *Engineers and Bildung*. In Christensen et.al. *Engineering Science, Skills and Bildung*. Aalborg. Aalborg University Press.

Lave, Jean & Wenger, Etienne, 1991. *Situated learning - Legitimate peripheral participation*. Cambridge. Cambridge University Press.

Schanz, Hans Jørgen, 1990. *Forandring og Ballance – Modernitet og metafysik (Change and Balance – Reflections on metaphysics and modernity)*. Århus. Modtryk.

Weinsheimer, Joel, 1985. *Gadamer's Hermeneutics*. New Haven. Yale University Press.

Ulla Thøgersen

Embodiment as the existential soil of practice
Philosophical reflections on the concept of practice as "doing"

Introduction
The two-year master programme in Learning and Organisational Change offered at Aalborg University is an example of an education, which in its own account is practice-orientated (See chapter 1). In the study programme the 9th semester is described in the following way: the students will engage in an empirical project work in which they develop their academic competences in interplay with a practice context. The intended learning outcome is – amongst others – that the students develop competences to apply the theoretical insights and methods learned during the previous year of education in relation to the specific practice. Hence, this education is in line with an idea that seems to be prevailing at the moment in relation to organising higher education at university level, namely that cooperation between universities and enterprises or other organisations should support practice-based learning processes which engage the students with "real" tasks or problems of the workplace.

The aim of this chapter is *not* to critically discuss the strengths and weaknesses in relation to practice-orientated organisation of university education; rather the aim is to look – in more detail – at the concept of practice from a philosophical perspective. The concept of practice receives a specific meaning in the example above. It mainly refers to a specific domain or setting away from the university, namely workplace practice outside the university walls. This displays the tendency to separate school (university) from the concept of practice. Taken to an extreme, what goes on in educational activities at universities is not practice; it can at most be *about* practice or more or less practice-orientated. This tendency can also be seen in the dichotomy of theory and practice. In the example above the concept of theory is mainly related to the university and the learning activities taking place here; whereas the concept of practice refers to the workplace context of real-life-problems in which theories can be applied or implemented. In this understanding the concepts of theory and practice point to two different forms of engagement in the world or display two different sorts of knowledge.

The philosophical interest in this chapter is to discuss the concept of practice in relation to a phenomenological understanding of embodied human existence (see e.g. Merleau-Ponty, 1945/1962; Welton, 1998, 1999). The chapter argues that we can get a more nuanced perspective on the relation of university and workplace within an educational setting *if* the concept of "practice" is not understood as one specific form of knowledge or engagement with the world related primarily to the workplace, but as a dynamic core in our existence linked to our general doing or in other words: to our way of living the world through an embodied engagement. This means that the concept of practice can refer to "doing" in the workplace setting, but at the same time it cannot be separated from the educational activities at the University. Practice is present in educational settings as well as in the workplace since both settings are bound to some form of doing and our embodied existence in general. Hence, this chapter argues against the tendency to take the concept of practice out of the university seminar rooms and auditoriums or at least the tendency to isolate the concept in its reference to workplace activities.

The focus on embodiment in relation to the concept of practice supports an idea of the similarity between workplace and educational settings. Instead of initially approaching the two settings by what sets them apart, what makes them different – e.g. in a distinction between theory and practice – the focus on embodiment brings them together in the perspective of the existential "soil" they have in common: in both settings we are engaged as embodied human beings. This is not to say that the differences between the two settings are not relevant to discuss, but the differences are only one side of the story. There are fundamental similarities to every setting or situation we engage in because of our embodied existence which we all as human beings have in common. This different starting point to understanding the relation of educational institution and workplace setting provides an alternative to the theory/practice-dichotomy and it underlines the primordial embodied engagement which is the ground of both settings.

In the following sections of this chapter the argument will be unfolded further drawing mainly on the phenomenology of Merleau-Ponty (1945/1992, 1964, 1974). The chapter is organised into four sections. The first section uses etymology and a short analysis of everyday language used to link the concept of practice to doing. The second section introduces the phenomenological perspective in order to understand embodiment as the existential "soil" of doing. These two sections set the two premises on which the further argument will be unfolded. The next section develops an understanding of embodiment as the existential "soil" of doing by focusing on the Merleau-Ponty's reflections on the lived body, e.g. by introducing his ideas on the permanence of the body and the intentional arc. The fourth concluding section returns to the concept of practice and highlights the argument carried out in the chapter.

Practice as "doing"

The first premise of this chapter is to (re)define or widen the concept of practice in relation to an understanding of "doing", namely to argue that we are always already partaking in practice at any moment in any situation as we are constantly "doing" the world. In this definition the concept of practice covers our doings in every situation and the concept becomes fundamental to how we understand and reflect on our own existence. Hence, it makes it problematic to view practice in the framework of being one specific form of engagement with the world only present in certain situations. No situation is devoid of practice.

This widening of the concept of practice goes back to the Latin root of the word in which "practico" means "to do". In everyday English language the word "practice" can have several meanings which in some way all refer to the activity of "doing", but the concrete meanings are more specific in its description of what is done. The word can be used as a verb: "to practice" in the sense of training by repetition, e.g. "I have to practice playing the piano to get good at it" or: "I am out of practice". This is linked to a second form of use in which the word "practice" describes a regular activity or manner of routine, e.g. "I practice yoga every Tuesday". And thirdly, it can be used to refer to specific domains of crafts or professions, e.g. to practice medicine, law or even more generally "practice" understood as carrying out work in general. A fourth form of use is already described above, namely the contrast of theory and practice – combined with the tendency to make theory an academic activity and practice an activity related to work settings. These different meanings of the word make the concept of practice refer to specific activities, but the commonality is that all the meanings refer back to an activity of doing something as such. In practice, while practicing I am doing something – it can be work, training etc., but the "ground" of practice lies in the verb of doing.

This chapter will – as suggested above – try to expand the concept of practice beyond its everyday meanings by focusing on practice as "doing" in a more general sense. Or: in other words, this chapter will focus on the similarity underlying every use of the concept of practice, namely that we are doing something. In its more particular argument this chapter will focus on embodiment as the existential soil underlying practice as "doing".

Embodiment as the existential soil of doing
A phenomenological perspective

The second premise of this chapter is that Merleau-Ponty's reflections on the lived body (le corps propre) in the *Phenomenology of Perception* can provide insights which are important to the development of a broader concept of practice as "doing" since his reflections bring forth the existential "soil" of our living in the world (Merleau-Ponty 1945/1962). It provides an account of the lived body as our general way of being engaged in the world and allows us to draw on this account in relation to a discussion of the intentionality of doing and hence the concept of practice.

Early on it should be noted, however, that Merleau-Ponty himself rarely uses the concept of practice. He talks of "doing" in several places, but he does not – like Bourdieu (1995, 1990) or de Certeau (1984) for example – take his departure from the concept of practice. In the *Phenomenology of Perception* his starting points are the concepts of body and perception. This does not mean that the concept of practice has no place in his philosophy or that it cannot be linked to his philosophy. This chapter aims to show how this can be done. The interesting perspective in this venture is to develop a nuanced and broad concept of practice, which builds on an explicit understanding of the lived body.[1] A broad concept of practice makes the arguments concerning practice-orientated education and the dichotomy of theory and practice possible, which are found in the beginning of this chapter. It should also be noted that these arguments can be found in similar formulations in learning theories such as Wenger (2001) and Schön (1983) which both focus explicitly on the concept of practice. In this respect, the overall argument as such might seem to offer nothing new to the field of learning theory, but what is new in the phenomenological approach is to discuss the concept of practice based on reflections of embodied existence and in this sense develop a strong link between practice and embodiment. Neither Wenger nor Schön have an eye for this link. Schön places his discussion of education within an understanding of how we frame and reframe the world around us. As such his understanding is much more cognitive orientated; even though he seems to presuppose the body in his description of how we "think on our feet". However, a concept of body is never elaborated in his theory. In relation to the definition of communities of practice Wenger mainly points to social processes of meaning, and he does not mention the body in his definition of practice. Merleau-Ponty's phenomenology is interesting in light of the missing concept of the body in Schön and Wenger as his philosophy offers a concept of the body which can be taken as the starting point for reflections on practice.

Phenomenology is to reflect on our lived experiences in order to characterise how we as humans are engaged in the world (see also Barbaras 2004, 1997; Dillon 1999, 1988; Pietersma 2000, Sokolowski 2000). One of Merleau-Ponty's main points is that we are essentially engaged in the lived world through our embodiment. As a challenge to both intellectualist (rational) and empiricist views on human existence Merleau-Ponty is orientated at the body as "the soil" of human existence, namely the body as the primordial site of experience and expression and hence the site of our "doings". In the *Phenomenology of Perception* Merleau-Ponty argues that we need to surpass a dualistic Cartesian understanding of the body as *res extensa* (an extended thing) and the mind as *res cogitans* (a thinking thing) since the lived experience of one's own body points to an incarnate intentionality which functions as a pre-reflective orientation towards the perceptual world (Merleau-Ponty 1945/1962). In other words: the body cannot be reduced to a biological mechanism which places us in objective space, but the body is lived existence; namely the situated "site" for all orientation in the world. Merleau-Ponty talks of the body as *le corps propre*, namely one's own lived body. The lived body is flesh, but the body as flesh continuously transcends itself and works as an "open system" for engagement into the world (Merleau-Ponty, 1945/1962).

Phenomenological philosophy has generally contested the idea that the concept of intention should be the starting point for inquiry into human existence. Instead phenomenology suggests the concept of intentionality which means that human existence is always already directed at something, but the direction does not have to be based on clear intentions behind an activity or be an incidental (non-intended) product of an intended activity (see Husserl 1999; Merleau-Ponty, 1945/1962). Our intentionality, our direction in the world, is bound to an open-ended process of meaning anchored in the dynamic interrelation of the individual and the lived (social) world. From this perspective a philosophical challenge is to understand how we as humans generally are engaged in the lived world through intentionality and how different forms of intentionality are at play and work together in our way of living the world.

The following section of the chapter will mainly focus on two aspects central to understanding the primordial "soil" of embodiment in human existence: a) the permanence of the body and b) the embodied intentional arc. These aspects will be used to underline the essential embodiment related to the intentionality of "doing" – and as such provide a perspective on the concept of practice.

The embodiment of human existence

Fundamental to phenomenology is the concept of phenomenon (Greek: phainómenon), namely 'that which appears in an experience'. In this sense phenomenology in general is interested in the study of how something appears to us in human existence. To Merleau-Ponty it is essential to argue that there is a primordial layer of our existence in which the phenomenon expresses the experiential appearance of the things themselves. Or more precisely: the phenomenon is the expression of the things-in-themselves-for-us. This formulation testifies to the intimate grip between humans and the world. As humans we constantly engage in the world through our experiences and as we live through situations, but the situations only appear, because the things in the world appear as a field of meaning in which we can engage and in their appearance the things carry their own premises for handling, their own claims for meaning, which in turn demands certain responses from us. As such our existence is based on being-in-the-world.

In his study of the primordial layer of existence in which the phenomenon is founded it is essential to Merleau-Ponty to direct embodiment. We engage in a situation through our existence as embodied. Hence, to Merleau-Ponty the body is significant in the answer to why anything appears to us at all and it is essential in understanding how the world is opened up as a temporal and spatial place in which we always already engage ourselves in situations. In other words, in his phenomenological reflections we find the body as a fundamental part of our own existence – not because the body as an organic system is what keeps us alive, but because the body is a nexus of meaning processes, the body is the core from which we approach the lived world.

These reflections bring to light a certain concept of the body, namely one's own lived body (le corps propre). The lived body is not the expression of the organic body, but a body, which carries the whole of our existence. Naturally the body can be described as an organic system, which functions according to principles of physiology and anatomy. I can look at my body as this organic "thing" and as such reflect on my body as something material, something with a certain solidity, which I can grab and hold. However, in this reflection I thematise the body as something *I have* and I create a distance to my own body. I have ears. I have eyes. From a phenomenological perspective this means that I hold back an experience of the immediate lived body and I begin to look at the body as a means to my presence in the world. As such this reflection overlooks the lived body as something *I am*, something which carries my existence, not only as organic life, but as an immediate engagement into the (social) world of meaning.

The lived body indicates that "I am body". For example, if I stand on a nail, I would not say that the foot is causing pain the same way the nail is. My pain points to the nail – and the immediate experience of pain testifies to the experience of the body as something other than an object to me (something I have); rather the body points to an identity: it is me. We find the same when we look at our movement. I do not have to localise my body somewhere in objective space before I move it, because the body is me. For example, at the moment of writing this sentence on the computer, I do not have to look for my body in order to move my fingers across the keyboard, but I move the fingers immediately, without medium, because the body is there as me. In being a body there is a natural certainty about an embodied presence, which points to my existence as an immediate embodied existence in which the body is there as the carrier of my engagement, of my doing. I walk without thinking about my legs. I talk without thinking about my lips. I am constantly directed at the world without reflecting on the body as a means to my contact with the world.

To understand how we generally are engaged in the world Merleau-Ponty turns to the permanence of the body. Merleau-Ponty argues that the lived body is the "here and now" of my existence in a spatial and temporal world. He connects this argument to what he calls the absolute permanence of my own body (Merleau-Ponty, 1945, pp. 106; 1962 pp. 90). My existence is bound to the fact that I *am* body. I cannot step out of the body, but the body is the place and the time from where I live and get to know the world. I cannot detach myself from my own body, but the (potential) appearance (and absence) of the things in the world depend on the primordial permanence of the body. The permanence of the body leads Merleau-Ponty to say that I view the world through an embodied perspective. He gives the example of a perception of a church through a window. I can only see parts of the church. The window, however, is relative permanent as I can move out of the room and hence I will see parts of the church, which were not visible through the window. However, I can never find a place where I can see *all* of the church at one time. My body also provides me with a perspective which I cannot escape. I can move around, but never seen the world from an all-encompassing view.

Merleau-Ponty describes how the perspective of the body is bound to the experience of situations, not positions. In the normal everyday life I do not mainly experience my body as something which occupies a particular position in space, e.g. that my feet are *there* on the floor or that my arm is resting *here* on the table, but I experience my body as situated engagement. I am always already engaged in the things around me in the world related to the tasks or meanings incorporated into the specific situation. In other words: the body does not stop at the line of my skin, but it is actually to be viewed as an "open system" which works as an engagement into lived situations. This is not the same as saying that I use my body as a medium for engagement into the world. This statement would imply that something other than the lived body is in control of the body, but I am immediately – without medium – engaged in the world. This also means that my attention does not have to be on the body and the use of it, but I *am* this body, which constantly directs itself towards the world and I am where there is something for me to do. In other words: I am always already "out" in the world engaged in the tasks, which unfolds as part of the situation.

An example: if I am at a café, then the café does not appear to me as geometric space telling me about my objective position in the world in relation to the objective space of the things in the café. Rather, the experience of space is linked to my situated embodied engagement. The café is spatial in the sense that it provides me with situations in which I can carry out specific actions. I can order coffee, read a paper, listen to music, talk to my friends, play backgammon etc. These are all possible actions for me, which I can carry out in the café. The café is experienced as situated space in which I always already act and express myself without having to think about my position and without having to find the different parts of my body to undertake certain actions. I am already engaged in the café as an immediate experienced situation by always already doing actions possible in this particular situation. Hence, Merleau-Ponty situates human existence in being-in-the-world and he points to a fundamental embodied intentionality, which has to do with a pre-objective engagement in the lived world.

As bodies we constantly project ourselves towards the lived world based on our habits and the actual 'challenges' related to the action at hand. The habitual body is the body which – based on past experiences – has acquired specific ways of relating to the world, certain habits, which constantly function as a habitual setting for the present action. The present body is the body here and now which draws on habits as certain familiar rhythms in our existence to engage in the actions at hand; however the present body may need to learn new ways of relating to the world if the world presents itself as an unfamiliar situation. Hence the temporality of the body plays an important role in the way we engage in the world and often our present actions, our engagement in situations, are spontaneous, immediate and intuitive in the sense of being based on the habitual body.

To sum up: to Merleau-Ponty our existence is based on the permanence of the body and the body as situated engagement – and our existence is based on temporal processes of habitual settings and the present tasks of the situation. He connects these reflections in what he calls the "intentional arc". He writes: *"the life of consciousness … is subtended by an 'intentional arc' which projects around us our past, our future, our human setting, our physical, ideological and moral situation, or rather which results in our being situated in all these respects. It is this intentional arc which brings about the unity of senses, of intelligence, of sensibility and motility."* (Merleau-Ponty, 1945, p. 158; 1962, p. 136). The intentional arc projects the lived world as situations around us and the concept expresses the primordial embodied intentionality which means that we are constantly engaged in the lived world. According to Merleau-Ponty, the intentional arc discloses our primordial intentionality as "I can" and "I do", rather than "I think". When situations are projected around me through the embodied intentional arc, then this projection is not carried out by an inner thinking consciousness, but by the body as already engaged in the world. Merleau-Ponty writes that motility is not first and foremost a matter of "I think", but "I can". Movement is not thought of or a representation of movement, but spontaneous movement which can be better described in sentences as "I can" or "I do": "I am not in space or time, nor do I conceive space and time; I belong to them, my body combines with them and includes them". (Merleau-Ponty, 1945, pp. 162; 1962, p. 140). The body is not "the servant of an inner consciousness", but it is the lived body, which answers the calls of the experienced things, for example lifting a fork or a glass at dinner, driving a car etc. It is the lived body, which by its movements apprehends the world by inhabiting it.

Merleau-Ponty talks of "understanding" in terms of an embodied grasp of meaning. He says that the body understands or *"has its world without having to make use of 'symbolic or 'objectifying function"* (Merleau-Ponty, 1945, p. 164; 1962, pp. 140). Our understanding of a lived situation does not reside in pure thought or in an objective body working according to causal mechanisms, but the lived body inhabits the meanings of the experienced things in the world and as such becomes our anchorage in the world. This is particularly visible with habits, e.g. I walk through the door without having to compare the width of the door to that of my body and I ride my bike without being able to formulate verbally what I am actually doing (Merleau-Ponty, 1945, p.167; 1962, p. 143; see also Schön, 1983). There is an immediate perceptual reliability based on an embodied knowing. Or in other words: there is a knowledge inhabited in our embodied being-in-the-world, which constantly functions in our situated experiences of the world.

These reflections mean that we are constantly "doing" the world. The intentionality of doing discloses itself as bound to the primordial embodied intentionality in which human existence is embodied being-in-the-world. In a broad sense the intentionality of doing carries our very way of constantly answering the challenges the world poses to us – or in other words: our way of being engaged in the situations around us. When this understanding of "I do" is related to the concept of practice, then it means that we are always engaged in practice. Every situation holds a dimension of practice because we are constantly engaging in situations and partake in actions on the basis of our situated engagement.

Conclusion

The notion of the lived body and the reflections on embodied existence and the intentionality of doing bring us back to the key arguments presented in the introduction of this chapter. The main argument is that the concept of practice is not one specific form of knowledge or engagement with the world related primarily to specific work settings (in contrast to theory as another form of knowledge). Practice, understood as the lived expression of our intentionality of doing, is a dynamic core in our embodied existence linked to our way of living the world through situated engagement. As such the concept of practice can express our doings in the workplace (work situations), but it equally expresses well our doings in other situations, e.g. in educational institutions. In this respect we cannot talk of practice in terms of more/less: "practice is more present in work settings than in educational settings." Practice is every present and each lived situation holds its own premises for practice related to the tasks at hand. As such it makes sense to talk of different forms of practice settings in the sense that our lives display different habits or routines connected to specific situations. The work setting qua its organisation and its specific tasks displays certain premises of the type of doings happening here – and the educational setting likewise holds its premises for the type of doings which takes place here. The concept of setting turns attention to the context of the practice and the certain demands of the context to act a certain way; but again it must be stipulated that one context cannot claim to be the carrier of practice alone. Or formulated differently: both workplace and educational settings are bound to practice.

This concept of practice highlights the similarities to every situation we are engaged in independent of the context: we are always already engaged in the situation through our embodied perspective and an intentional arc. In this sense, instead of approaching work setting and educational settings by what sets them apart, the focus is turned to the individual embodied existence, which is the carrier of practice per se. The existential "soil" of every situation, of practice, is embodied human existence. This perspective means that we have to approach different settings of practice from the focus of being body, namely from the premise that we are – as humans – always already immediate bodies living the world.

Notes
1 It would be interesting to discuss how the concept of practice developed on the basis of Merleau-Ponty's phenomenology distinguishes itself from the concepts of practice found in Bourdieu and de Certeau; however this discussion is not unfolded here and will have to be the topic of another chapter.

References

Barbaras, Renaud, 2004. *The Being of the Phenomenon. Merleau-Ponty's ontology.* Bloomington, USA. Indiana University Press,

Barbaras, Renaud, 1997. *Merleau-Ponty. La collection: Philo-philosophes.* Paris, France. Ellipses.

Bourdieu, Pierre, 1990. *The logic of practice.* Stanford University Press.

Bourdieu, Pierre, 1995. *Outline of a theory of practice.* Cambridge University Press.

de Certeau, Michel, 1984. *The Practice of everyday life.* University of California Press.

Dillon, Martin (eds.), 1991. *Merleau-Ponty Vivant.* Albany, USA. SUNY Press.

Dillon, Martin, 1988. *Merleau-Ponty's Ontology.* Bloomington, USA. Indiana University Press.

Husserl, Edmund, 1999. *The idea of phenomenology.* The Netherlands. Kluwer Academic Publishers.

Merleau-Ponty, Maurice, 1974. *The primacy of Perception and its Philosophical Consequences.* In: O'Neill, John (eds.), 1974. *Phenomenology, language and perception. Selected essays of Maurice Merleau-Ponty.* London, England. Heinemann Educational Books Ltd.

Merleau-Ponty, Maurice, 1964. *Sense and Non-sense.* Evanston, Illinois, USA. Northwestern University Press.

Merleau-Ponty, Maurice, 1962. *Phenomenology of Perception.* London, Great Britain. Routledge & Kegan Ltd.

Merleau-Ponty, Maurice, 1945. *Phénoménologie de la Perception.* Paris, France. Gallimard.

Pietersma, Henry, 2000. *Phenomenological Epistemology.* Oxford, UK. Oxford University Press.

Schön, Donald, 1983. *The Reflective Practitioner: How professionals think in action.* London, UK. Temple Smith.

Sokolowski, Robert, 2000. *Introduction to Phenomenology.* Cambridge, UK. Cambridge University Press.

Welton, Donn (eds.), 1999. *The Body. Classic and Contemporary readings.* London, UK: Blackwell Publishers.

Welton, Donn (eds.), 1998. *The Body and Flesh. A Philosophical Reader.* London, UK: Blackwell Publishers.

Wenger, Etienne, 2001. *Communities of practice: Learning, meaning and identities.* Cambridge, UK: Cambridge University Press.

Lars Botin

PBL and stories of body in the hospital world

This story/stories of how I moved around in the hospital world for a limited time should be read as emergent, "subjective" and personal, and based on structured feelings and experiences, but at the same time I try to use established, scientific procedures that are at the very basis of any kind of questioning, story-telling or investigation of a problem. Throughout the chapter I shall discuss how and why cultural analysis and body could have a say and a meaning in relation to considering a technological problem where techniques, organizations and people are in a process of change.

The current status of EHRs (Electronic Health Records) in the Danish health care system is far from perfect as regions and decision-makers try to deal with the various technical, economic and organizational problems. My investigation of EHRs has focused on what might be termed the human aspects. By making video-observations of the use of EHRs in particular settings, I have tried to identify some of the human factors involved, and in particular, see how the human relations, especially communication, in the hospital have been affected. My emphasis has been on the body and, not least, the "body-language" that can be observed through a video camera.

Presenting the problem

"She looked at the screen on the wall showing a brand new interface of a trial model of an electronic health record. She sighed almost ecstatically and moved her body forwards on the chair as she exclaimed: "This is beautiful, why didn't we have this from the very beginning".

We were at the end of the trial period (3 months) and finally the computer department at the hospital had managed to create something that all of the participants at the conference approved and appreciated. She was the only one expressing out loud what she thought of the interface, but everybody else in the room were moved by her words and body language.

She looked at the screen and was puzzled by the various layers of meaning and expression in the representation of the patient that was lying next to her. For many minutes she interacted with the screen seeking counseling from the nurse standing behind her. She tapped in information in various columns and boxes in the schemes of the record and paid very little attention to the patient in bed. Some times she would ask the patient for information, but she would not look at her or revolve her bodily attention towards the patient in bed. The ward-visit ended and the doctor had spent more time than usual in the consultation, but less time in interacting with the patient in bed.

She looked in a very perplexed way at the screen and shouted out loud: "The patient has disappeared!"! It stood clear that the patient she was about to visit had vanished from the screen and despair was at hand. She tried to phone the ICT department, but they were busy elsewhere and then she tried to involve a 'super-user' (a nurse) in order to solve the problem. Meanwhile the patient was lying just a few meters away and was able to overhear the conversation and probably understand the problem. She had disappeared! The problem was solved (by miracle it seems) 15 minutes later and the ward-round could move on".

These are three events that actually took place as I recently followed a ward-round at a hospital in Denmark. In the midst of the situation I was not aware of what was going on. The events taking place seemed pretty harmless and quite straightforward, and it was not until I began video editing the observations that I had made that I reflected upon the meaning and importance of the events. I had documented the situations on a video-camera and the force of the pictures became apparent as I looked through the material that I had recorded together with colleagues.

I began to wonder why apparently emphatic doctors and nurses would "forget" the patient on behalf of virtual representations on a screen, and why no one in representing the final edition of the video-observations seemed to notice what I thought was a major problem: How could doctors and nurses forget the physical patient?

I began to ask questions and wonder and I think that this wondering and has to do with my training as a researcher, teacher and supervisor in a problem-based learning environment.

Problem-based learning, or PBL

PBL (problem-based learning) and related research perceives reality in terms of problems to be solved. It originally grew out of an action-oriented approach to research and education where science, technology and human affairs are seen as intertwined, entangled and interactive. At its best it tends toward interdisciplinary, transgender, cross cultural interaction and methodologically it makes use of case-studies, be they singular or multiple.

PBL is concerned with all the aspects of the classical Aristotelian division of knowledge in *episteme, techné and phronesis*, but with an emphasis, as I see it, on *phronesis* and *techné*. The classical problem of whether scientific and technological innovations should take place or not is not relevant in terms of *episteme,* but is crucial if we look at the problem from a *phronetic* point of view.

By emphasizing the humanistic and societal aspect of PBL I go along with the original idea of the so-called Aalborg model concerning PBL, which can be summarized in the following quotation by Knud Illeris: "The crucial aspect in PBL is that it does not take a stand in disciplines that have been constituted in the past and were a result of bygone societal relations and constructions, but deals with actual problems by applying relevant knowledge, theories and methods from the disciplines". (Illeris 1974, p. 80) (my adapted translation).

In this perspective Bent Flyvbjerg has, in a PBL context, drawn a synthetic scheme that might help us to understand the importance of values and interests as we produce knowledge and technology.

Flyvbjerg identifies the field of *techné* as being where concrete problems of the real are located, and we can approach the "technical" field from two opposite positions, either from theories and laws or from values and interests.

Flyvbjerg claims that it is in the realm of *techné*, where theories and laws and analysis of values and interests are translated into practical activity that we find "how things ought to be done". (Flyvbjerg 1988, p. 60) The notion of "ought" is a distinct phronetic/ethical term, which Flyvbjerg readily admits. In translating this into a problem based research-method Flyvbjerg made the following list of recommendations:

- stay close to reality
- emphasize details and context
- f• ocus on everyday life
- s• tudy specific cases

- investigate what and how on behalf of why: tell stories
- focus on actors and structure

In the present study of problems in the healthcare sector I have tried to follow the recommendations made by Flyvbjerg and have stressed the importance of reality, everyday life, context, narratives and dialogue (communication). I have been concerned with PBL and knowledge production in a mainly engineering educational context, which is traditionally based on a hypothetical and deductive way of dealing with knowledge, hence relating to the epistemic and theoretical forms of knowledge. In this view the objects and products are seen as a result of prior construction of hypotheses and of testing in models that are based in theory. Theories and hypotheses are in this perspective considered as value-free and neutral, which means that the results and products cannot be otherwise. Objects, artifacts and technologies have no meaning or "identity" that goes beyond what is found in the objective theoretical construction.

In the course of my research I have come to realize that knowledge can never be value-free when people are involved, since people have interests and agendas that cannot be disregarded or ignored. In a PBL context this becomes even more apparent, because a problem is *something* for *somebody*. In engineering *something* is an existing (or future existing) object that is (or will become), which means that it is crucial to consider the problem solution process with regard to the problem as being real and there for somebody to consider, act upon and eventually reflect upon.

In doing this it becomes clear that problems are more than hypothetical and deductive in their essence, and what should be striven for (in accordance to the recommendations made by Illeris and Flyvbjerg) is an approach that seriously and critically considers the societal and cultural potential and possibilities in any problem solution.

In this perspective product, artifact and object become bearers of a societal and cultural identity, which makes it so that we should be able to reflect upon that identity. It is obvious that this kind of reflection has very little to do with the hypothetical and deductive method, and considers the things in a constant process of making where a multiple core of variables influence the outcome of the process. The affluences and influences are layered in the object forming a character of identity, which according to the interests, values, involved actors and contextual layering can be seen and understood as technical, functional, aesthetic, material and so forth. In any case there can be no doubt, seen from this particular PBL perspective that objects have a say (by being embedded in the process, the history and the actors involved) and the stories that they tell cannot be heard and understood in a meaningful way unless we focus on processes, history and the actors themselves.

Approaching these concepts in a theoretical scientific way it becomes imperative to investigate the problem from different angles than the laboratory and model based reality of hard-core engineering.

Theoretical background

Evidence is what appears clearly and unmistakably in front of our eyes, and the tales told on the basis of evidence are radically different than those told on the basis of hypothesis and conjecture. Evidence is in its essence unquestionable and beyond dispute, and concrete and corresponding statements can be made on behalf of evidence. Statements concerning evidence can be transferred and translated, and therefore it seems quite natural that a system, like electronic health records (EHR), which tends toward general and universal classification and standardization revolves its attention toward evidence as the main way for controlling the undertakings and on-goings within the system. Evidence is at the same time tied up in the "lens-paradigm" of Western science and culture, hence relating to theory and observation as scientific background. At the same time evidence is also tied up upon pragmatics, which means that practices, procedures and processes in the system that seems to function and work are embraced by evidence. This pragmatic use and reading of the concept is although constantly challenged by the scientific paradigm of medicine and Evidence Based Medicine (EBM) is increasingly becoming based on clinical evidence of scientific and analytical value (Sackett et. al., 1996).

The ground structure for electronic health records in the Danish health care system is envisioned in a PBL rationale, but the disciplinary emphasis in modern medicine on evidence is to a large extent incompatible with the current PBL approach, because the latter, in my reading, goes beyond the mere concrete and evidential.

Recently, Michael Hård and Andrew Jamison, in their book *Hubris and Hybrids. A Cultural History of Technology and Science* (2005) have tried to take a cultural approach by looking what they term "sites of cultural appropriation" where technology and science are actually put to use in society. No meaningful and useful technical artifact is purely based on empirical and analytical scientific procedure, but entails human endeavors, intentions, experiences and processes of creative appropriation, which are, to a large extent, based on our cultural values and traditions, as well as our *"body skhemas"*. Merleau Ponty's notions on embodiment are dealt with in an other chapter in this volume therefore I shall only give a short summary of the *body skhema* in my perspective:

- General quality and capacity of the human body (aesthetics).
- Common attitude and perception of the body (ethics).
- Universal and cyclical perception of time and space, hence fusion of past, present and future (experienced physics).

Hård and Jamison are certainly far from phenomenological in their approach but in the stories they tell, they complement the more abstract philosophical notions of Martin Heidegger in showing that: "there is nothing technological about technology". In any case, they provide a number of concepts and examples by which we can consider technology as something other than technical, showing how users become co-constructors or innovators; by the ways they appropriate technology into their lives.

Hård and Jamison write in their conclusions that our analyses and explanations of technology have become ever more specialized, fragmented and domain-dependent, hence obstructing a deeper and more holistic understanding of the ways and means of technology: "a historically oriented cultural assessment of technoscience requires that we tell new stories of the past, stories that can transcend the polarization between romance and tragedy" (Hård and Jamison 2005, p. 294). This means that we need to break down the boundaries between hard-core natural science and soft-core human science in order to truly understand the socio-technical "hybrids" that have emerged from the combinations of science, technology, economics and society.

Neither wholly heroic nor completely tragic the stories of science and technology need to reflect the ambiguities and ambivalences that characterize our human interaction with our technical things. In order to do that we have to "look elsewhere" so to say than merely into the technical, professional and/or disciplinary history of for instance medicine, because the latter will give us only uncritical and primarily heroic narratives focussing on progress and evolution. Hård and Jamison write: "Cultural historians, however, tend to be highly critical toward such all-encompassing and congratulatory stories. In contrast, they attempt to uncover alternative stories, "small narratives, that not only view the past from other perspectives but also represent less grandiose, more mundane events" (Hård and Jamison 2005, p. 304-05).

In considering the terms introduced by Hård and Jamison in *Hubris and Hybrids. Cultural Appropriation of Technology* (2005) on this more contextual level we find *internalization* as crucial for the cultural appropriation of technology and science.

Internalization on a phenomenological level has to do with embodiment and experience that goes beyond intellectual verbalization. In the words of E.M. Bruner: "As social scientists we have long given too much weight to verbalizations at the expense of images. Lived experience, then, as thought and desire, as word and image, is the primary reality." (Bruner 1986, p. 5) Our interactions with technologies on a lived experiential level have to do with "emotions, values, ideals and strong feelings" (McCarthy and Wright, 2004, p. 2) which are difficult to embrace and explain on a scientific level, but as science and technology are touching and concerning our everyday life and we understand our lives and existence through our everyday life, then we have to find concepts, terms and methods for enhancing and promoting the importance of experience and cultural appropriation. The proposition of this chapter is that in supplementing and complementing already existing concepts, terms and methods for understanding the impact and use of technology we have to turn our attention toward culture and body, because: "Technology in the contemporary world involves cultural values, ideologies, ethical concerns; it is also shaped by political and economic determinants" (Murphy and Potts, 2003, p. 4).

We relate to the outer world, as Merleau Ponty points out, of technological problems and potentials through our bodies and these bodies are multiple and in order to a grip on the complexity of problems and potentials we have to take into consideration all of these bodies.

The American philosopher Mark Johnson has distinguished five bodies that interact with the world in slightly different ways. I have chosen to present the five bodies in the following list and briefly comment on their essential qualities.

1. The biological body: The conglomeration of flesh, bone, organs, skin and liquids that makes the body an object in time and space would be the definition of the natural scientist, but Johnson places more meaning into the body as a biological organism. The above mentioned elements that constitute the biological body "makes possible the qualities, images, feelings, emotions, and thought patterns that constitute the ground of our meaning and understanding" (Johnson 2007, p. 276). Our biological bodies are not outside ourselves or our brains, but actively engaged in creating

meaning and understanding through the *body skhema*, as described by Merleau Ponty.
2. The ecological body: If we demarcate the environment and the body then it is an artificial and constructed division due to our interests and values. "…we must think of organism (or body) and environment in the same way that we must think of mind and body, as aspects of one continuing process" (Johnson 2007, p. 276). There is no real distinction between body and environment, and the efforts made within dualistic and analytical science fail to see that if such a distinction is made, then both environment and body will suffer.
3. The phenomenological body: "This is our body as we live it and experience it" (Johnson 2007, p. 276). Johnson talks about a *body image* which is generated within us as we move, act and perceive in time and space. The image: "capture our reflexive and self-referential perceptions, attitudes, and beliefs of our bodies at this phenomenological level (Johnson 2007, p. 276). The *body image* is hence interdependent with the *body skhema*, and if we are to take the considerations made by Johnson seriously there is not a hierarchical relationship between the two, just a higher degree of reflection at stake as we live our phenomenological bodies.
4. The social body: Johnson is very brief concerning the qualities of our social bodies and writes: "We are who we are in and through others and by virtue of our intersubjective capacity to communicate shared meanings" (Johnson 2007, p. 277) The essence of the short description is that there is a certain overlap with the ecological body, and it is hard to understand why Johnson divides the context into environmental and social.
5. The cultural body: Besides dividing the context into physical and social he introduces cultural context: artifacts, practices, rituals, institutions and modes of interaction. (Johnson 2007, p. 277) Our bodies are to some extent culturally constructed but "the reduction of the body to the mere physical organism is just as misguided as the opposite error of claiming that the body is nothing but a cultural construction" (Johnson 2007, p. 277).

I think that the quintessential body as pictured by Johnson could be reduced to a three dimensional body, without losing meaning or clarity. The context *is* physical, social and cultural; and how the body interacts and interplays with these 'different' kinds of contexts are not essentially different; as can be seen as well from the analyses made by Johnson. We might act on a more sensorial and physical level with the ecological environment; and on a more reflective (phenomenological) level with our social and cultural surroundings, but in my opinion this division, and to some extent as well hierarchical levelling, leaves the body behind on behalf of imagining and reflection. In fact Johnson seems to place mind over body, which was certainly not his intention. Nevertheless I find the list useful in mapping the body in its various qualities and potentials, as well as the notion made by Johnson of not reducing body into a physical organism nor a cultural construction, but to embrace the body as a revealer and bearer of identity and self that goes beyond the flesh and incorporates- embodies - cultural and social attitudes.

Body and technology in the hospital system.

The video material at hand covering a morning-session before the introduction of a trial EHR and material that covers a morning-session after the introduction of a trial EHR. The figures present in the two sessions are more or less the same, with the exception of the ward-nurse. This means that we can actually make a comparison between the two sessions concerning time, space, technology, and attitude and behaviour of the actors in play.

In the session before introduction of the EHR it is quite apparent that everybody has fairly routine-like attitude towards the various common spaces in which they find themselves. There is a certain flow of communication and interaction, which mainly deals with papers and documents that circulates around the paper-journal. The doctor has a daily practice of ripping paper into halves at the morning conference, because she obviously likes that format (A5) and it probably means that the paper is easier to fit into her pocket. At the morning-conference there is a certain kind of movement and interaction as the conference moves on, because everybody has a say and a role concerning the procedures of each patient. The therapist knows about procedures for rehab for the singular patient, and she tells everybody else in the room, whilst the doctor nods her head. And in the end a unanimous decision will be made and registered on the white-board concerning further procedure.

It was quite evident during the take that things and bodies were moved in time and space as the conference moved on, and there was a lot of talking going on. The morning conference finishes at 8.50 AM sharp, because at this point the doctor normally keeps her morning-break and drinks her coffee and eats some bread, in order to be ready to prepare more thoroughly for the ward-round. As she considers the various amounts and kinds of medicine that each patient should be given she pauses and looks at a picture on the wall. She talks to the camera saying that in the future she will probably not be given the chance to think whilst writing, because it will be a matter of filling in boxes and changing a pair of digits. She is a bit frightened about this, but ends up saying that the time spared on this behalf will provide more time to the patient and probably she will find other ways and procedures for thinking whilst acting.

The ward-round is a 2 ½ hour session that covers the visitation of 25 patients, which means that there is approximately 6 minutes on average for each patient. As everything is in place, concerning the paper-journal before entering into the room there is very little time consumed in the handling of the papers and the journal, as doctor, nurse and patient are interacting and communicating for a relatively brief period of time. It was the experience at the ward-round before the trial EHR that the doctor would place the paper-journal on the foot-side of the bed and move towards the patient and ask how she/he was doing. During the conversation the doctor would eventually pick up the journal and explain the more precise and quantitative aspects of the ongoing care and treatment. The bodily directedness of the doctor and the nurse was obviously interrelational, as they interacted with the patient and amongst themselves.

If we look at the situation after the introduction of a trial EHR then we see a different picture concerning interaction and communication between staff, and furthermore between staff and patient. All the staff was as emphatic and in good mood as during the 1st take, so changes could not be ascribed to a different mood, but probably to the introduction of the technology.

It became apparent from first sight that all types of information-technology were in play, despite the fact that the EHR was meant to replace personal noteblocks, the nurse-cardex and the paper-jourrnal. Illustration 1 shows how a nurse is handling, at the same time, three different types of technologies – her own personal notebook, a more official cardex and the EHR, making cross-references and duplicating from one media to another.

If we look at the two places in question, the nurse group-room and the conference-room, then considerable change is visible. The lap-top and the images on the screen are gradually eliminating interaction and communication, as nurses sit on their own and the doctor is navigating the crew from the centre of the room by the aid of the computer.

Even if the computer has become crucial it is not replacing the other types of information-technology, which the images and the video-

Ill. 1. *The nurse is handling three information-technologies at the same time.* (Botin, 2004).

Referring and duplicating data from one media to another. She is sitting alone, which was emblematic to the situation after introduction of a trial EHR. Interaction and communication with colleagues and peers diminished radically, if we look into the nurses' group-room.

movie show very distinctly. Staff is now supposed to handle much more data and technology than before, and it is quite symptomatic that the doctor ends up saying that the conference only took 10 minutes longer than before introduction of a trial EHR. We are talking about a very small unit of 30 beds and that particular day there were only 21 occupied beds in the ward, so probably it was due to the coverage of beds that delay had been shortened compared to other days in the trial period.

In illustration 2 we are still at the conference and I have chosen the image because I find it fairly emblematic for the whole discussion. In the middle we see the doctor, surrounded by technology, manipulating the computer. She is looking down as if in control of the device and ready to move on to the next step. She is as well surrounded by staff; in this case the ward-nurse, a therapist and a secretary, and they are all moved by the commands of the navigator as their whole attention is directed towards the projection on the wall. They are presented to a new interface of the trial model, and they are all expressing enthusiasm and the nurse says it is fantastic. What they are looking at is a traditional screen-image that resembles an excel screen, with columns and rows,

PBL and Stories of Body in the Hospital World

Ill. 2. *At the end of the conference the doctor presents a new screen-interface and all of the staff is literally moved and taken by the 'beauty' of interface.* (Botin, 2004).

The doctor, as a captain on a ship, is navigating, surrounded by technology, the staff that physically follows her commands from the screen.

which makes it hard for an outsider to understand the immediate enthusiasm, because the interface was not even tried out. We are talking about a mere presentation of a representation, where no interaction took place, and as such the mere static representation managed to overwhelm and capture the viewers in place, from nurse to secretary. The force of the iconic, geometrical figure is, as can be seen, impressive.

At the conference the staff gets ready for the ward-round and some of the following procedures of ordering papers and data in order to meet the patient was of course eliminated by the new procedures, which means that the ward-round began more or less at the same time as before although some of the staff had to cut their morning-coffee break. The set-up for the ward-round was pretty impressive with mobile wagons carrying both lap-top and paper-journals.

It seemed as if this new set-up of mixed media also mixed up and jammed procedures, because at almost every visitation there were problems of finding data, either the physical ones on paper or the digital ones on the screen. The "movie" shows quite clearly how nurse and doctor are frustrated over the missing paper-journal, which is found after 10 minutes of search lying on top of the wagon managed by the doctor! A similar frustration is at hand as a patient disappears in cyberspace and they cannot find her on the screen. The nurse says that it often happens; and that the problem has not been solved yet by the IT department. Another 10 minutes passes by whilst the IT department finds the patient in the system. Meanwhile the whole communication, which takes place in the corridor, is quite loud and both doctor and nurse exclaim that XX has disappeared, whilst the patient in flesh and blood is lying 10 feet away listening to their communication.

The last sequence to mention concerning how body is absorbed by technology, deals with a visitation where the doctor and the nurse are totally engaged with the computer and hardly pay any attention to the patient. The wagon is rolled into the room and the doctor sits down in front of the computer. She is placed in a perpendicular angle to the patient lying in bed, very similar to the position she had before introduction of the new technology. But whereas the paper-journal was placed in the bed and only consulted a few times during visitation, then the slightly different position in the new set-up makes it so that the doctor is looking away from the patient and that the directedness of her body is turned towards the wagon and the computer. The doctor talks to the patient, but rarely looks at the patient, because she is busy typing and filling in columns and rows in the EHR.

Fig. 1. Conceptual sketch of how clinical actors are caught by the digital setting of the ward-round. (Botin, 2007).

The patient is lying in bead on the left side, whereas the doctor and nurse are concentrating on the lap-top on the right side. This was of course not the physical out-line of neither subjects, objects nor space, but an interpretation 'in situ' of what was actually going on.

All the attention of the doctor is directed towards the virtual patient on the screen and she interacts with this patient; which of course is a representation of the patient, but only a partial and virtual replica of what/who is lying in bed. The nurse is bending over the shoulder of the doctor and never engages with the patient as she mutely and with hands folded on her back follows the occurrences on the screen. The example evokes the experiences of the Canadian philosopher and sociologist A.W. Frank as he fell ill and was treated in the Canadian health care system: "Real diagnostic work takes place away from the patient; bedside is secondary to screen side. For diagnostic and even treatment purposes, the image on the screen becomes the 'true' patient, of which the bedridden body is an imperfect replica, less worthy of attention. In the screen simulations our initial certainty of the real (the body) becomes lost in hyper-real images that are better than the real body" (Frank 1991, p. 83)

We learned during the 1st and 2nd takes that the staff of the ward was highly empathetic to patients, relatives and colleagues, which means that this absorption and negligence could only be ascribed to the technology and not to changes in their personalities. We feel assured that these findings would not have become apparent if the actors were asked to reflect upon this in questionnaires and interviews, and at the same time it is even unsure if the images shown to the staff made them reflect upon this.

I think that the force of the pictures is quite striking in this regard and that phenomenological video-observation, where we look into the directedness of bodies in time and space in order to gain knowledge concerning interaction and communication, has shown potentials and qualities that complements and supplements other methods for observation.

Findings

The main results of the cases that were investigated in the Danish hospital system in relation to introduction of EHR, can be presented in the following way:

- The management, organizational and bureaucratic language at the upper level, contaminated by acronyms and abbreviation, make the language and communication incomprehensible to the other actors in the field. This means that the healthcare providers are more "knowing", than the actors (patients, secretaries and nurses) at a lower level in the hierarchy. The transfer of data, from one box to another is increasingly made through intermediaries who are more aware of the actual meaning of the message than the receiver.

- All actors in the field are to some extent familiar with one common tool – language – but the specific vocabulary is limited hierarchically. In the development of digital communication through computational devices, the software and hardware are accessible to only a few actors in the field. Shutters and barriers are ever more governing the direction of electronic systems for reasons that may be thought beneficial, i.e. in order to protect the patient's confidentiality perhaps. But the result is that communication and interaction is restricted and power is placed in a few hands following a prescribed hierarchy.
- There are widespread attempts to replace paper records by EHR. Paper records can be chaotic and can be manipulated at all levels, but there is transparency. It can, in principle, be accessed by even the "lowest" actor in the health care system. In contrast, the architecture of the new electronic patient record is hierarchal designed, which means that information is restricted as it gets more confidential, not necessarily to the benefit of the patient. This means that the EHR is turning into a black-box comparable to the way we produce engines for automobiles today. Once a mechanic was able to repair/interact with an engine with a wide repertoire of possible decisions. He could even put non-authorized items in the engine to make it function. Today the auto-mechanic orders authorized spare parts from the company and is increasingly less knowledgeable about the overall user function of the engine and its total construction. One might fear that the same evolution will take place as EHR records are constructed where actors are increasingly left out of the design of the system, and power is in the hands of administrations and system-developers.
- The study has shown that the self-understanding of the lifeworlds in the healthcare organization and the alleged "objective" reality do not fit, with severe consequences for both staff and patients. One way of addressing this problem is to document and communicate the extent of the mismatch. The phenomenological and iconographical video-observation has value in this respect because it is immediate and situated. The phenomenological and iconographical video observation is a strong tool, because it is directed, empathetic and seeking authenticity in what it reveals. It enhances the nuanced richness of context and reality, whereas detached video observation does not take into account the way in interactivity and communication are key avenues of human and technological interactivity.
- The study also shows that communication and interaction within the professional order, i.e. clinical communication, takes place in an-

other way than the actual system and the ongoing construction of EHR, tries to reflect. The organization is not a hierarchical and systemic gestalt, with fixed laws and rules for communication and interaction. The methodological approach to the subject matter exposes this very aspect and the value of the investigative tool (video) is enhanced by the ontological foundations of the method.

- The study demonstrates the value of emphasising subjectivity and intentionality and need for design to be driven by human intentionality as it is revealed in reality, driven by intentions based on values and what Merleau Ponty calls *skhema* (holdings). In doing this we are trying to emphasise ideas and values in order to engage in a dialogue. It might never turn into an objective given thing and as such legitimised, or becoming a fact, but I am willing and in place (*Dasein*, as Heigegger would have it).

Perspectives and concluding remarks

The study set out in emphasizing the importance of PBL in approaching situations and events of the present, because the core issue of PBL is to find solutions, potentials and possibilities of the actual and situated. I have tried to stress the fact that technical or theoretical solutions to problems have shown themselves to be problematic, and have drawn on perspectives concerned with cultural aspects of techniques and institutions/organizations, social consciousness, *body skhema* and hybrids as antidotes to hubris (Hård and Jamison, 2005). I think we have to find a way that stresses the potential in facing problems, which means we have to be pro-active, imaginative and positive in our approach. This means that we have to admit to science the capacity of producing human value and of art to be able to say something general and trustworthy (Mumford 1952, p. 140).

My study shows that PBL is in need of a "retouch", opening up for what could be called a field of in-between or hybridization (Hård and Jamison, 2005; Jamison, Christensen and Botin, 2011) where science and values/interests plays an equal part, where our various bodies could find potentials and possibilities for evolvement and improvement, becoming learning and understanding creatures by the aid and means of technology. It is in the in-between or the hybridization that the potentiality of problems in open-ended solutions really shows and on that account it would be worthwhile to dwell for a moment at the thoughts of Gilles Deleuze and Felix Guattari concerning the potency of the in-between.

The middle is in general considered as a calm and quiet realm in between extremes. I envision the middle, or the in between, as do Deleuze and Guattari as they state in a *Thousand Plateaus* (1980):

> "A rhizome has no beginning or end; it is always in the middle, between things, interbeing, *intermezzo*......... The middle is by no means an average; on the contrary, it is where things pick up speed. *Between* things does not designate a localizable relation going from one thing to the other and back again, but a perpendicular direction, a transversal movement that sweeps one and the other way, a stream without beginning or end that undermines its banks and picks up speed in the middle". (Deleuze and Guattari 1980/2007, p. 28).

It is in the in between where dynamic reflection and metamorphosis takes place and the drive is infused by objective and analytical scrutiny and phenomenological subjectification. The Hungarian artist and important member of Bauhaus Lazslo Moholy Nagy claimed this to be the essence of human endeavour: "We cannot establish a universal intellectual attitude or cultural standard from one vantage point only, such as cognition by means of logic, or the sciences, nor indeed from the arts exclusively. In order to form a comprehensive attitude to existence, we must start *simultaneously* from emotion and cognition." (Passuth 1982, p. 320)

Problems are in this perspective in between the ideal and the real, and of the world and reality. It is our perception and conception of potentials, possibilities, frictions and break-downs that constitute problems, which means that problems are not ideal or of the world, but exactly placed in between reality, which is subjective, and the world which is existing beyond our knowledge and objective.

In understanding this dynamic position and meaning of problems we find that in order to learn we have to take a multiple, simultaneous and inter-disciplinary perspective where cultural studies have an equal importance to social and scientific studies.

References
Bruner, Jerome, 1986. *Actual Minds, Possible Worlds*. Cambridge, MA. Harvard University Press.
Deleuze, Gilles and Guattari, Felix, 1980/2007. *A Thousand Plateaus*. London/New York. Continuum.

Flyvbjerg, Bent, 1988. *Aktuelle tendenser i videnskabsteori og byplanlaegning. (Actual tendencies in theories of science and town planning).* Aalborg. Aalborg University (working-paper).

Frank, Arthur. W., 1991. *At the Will of the Body: Reflections on Illness.* Boston/ New York. Houghton Mifflin.

Jamison, Andrew, Christensen Steen H. and Botin, Lars, 2011. *A Hybrid Imagination. Science and Technology in Cultural Perspective.* London; Claypool & Morgan Publishers

Hård, Mikael and Jamison, Andrew, 2005. *Hubris and Hybrids. A Cultural History of Technology and Science.* New York. Routledge

Illeris, Knud, 1974. *Problemorientering og deltagerstyring. (Problem-orientation and guidance of participation).* Roskilde. Roskilde Universitetsforlag.

Johnson, Mark, 2007. *The Meaning of the Body. Aesthetics of Human Understanding.* Chicago/London. The Chicago University Press.

McCarthy, John and Wright, Peter, 2004. *Technology as Experience.* Cambridge (MA). MIT Press.

Mumford, Lewis, 1952. *Art and Technics.* New York. Columbia University Press.

Murphie, Andrew and Potts, John, 2003. *Culture and Technology.* New York. Palgrave Macmillan.

Passuth, Krisztina, 1985. *Moholy Nagy.* London. Thames and Hudson.

Sackett, D. L. et. al., 1996. "*Evidence based medicine: what it is and what it is not*" in British Medical Journal, 1996, 312: 71.

Merete Wiberg

Inquiry in the swampy lowland

Introduction
In many study programmes within the area of higher education an internship is included. The aim of this chapter is to discuss what kind of learning environment an internship might offer when it comes to the student's ability to get hold of problematic situations. In order to analyse and discuss students learning of this ability in an internship context, Dewey's concept of inquiry will be applied due to its offer of a conceptualisation of learning processes in practice.

On an internship the student gets practical work experience by being situated in a real workplace setting where problematic situations are not designed for learning but are situations the student might meet in her future professional practice. One important challenge in a professional practice is to get hold of problematic situations in terms of defining and solving problems. Problematic situations might be anything from communication problems in an organisation, a machine that does not work properly or just something indefinite that gives a symptom but hides the reason, such as an unfriendly atmosphere in an organisation that influences the employees or a technical system that does not work. Dewey described 'problematic' as covering '..features that are designated by such adjectives as confusing, perplexing, disturbed, unsettled, indecisive..' (Dewey & Bentley, 1989 p. 282). The concept of inquiry offers a conceptualisation of how to get from a problematic situation to a situation which is possible to cope with. Dewey characterised the process as a transformation from an uncertain situation to a situation which appears as a coherent whole. In the process of transformation, symbols are applied in order to establish relationships within the situation and by means of these constitute a coherent whole. In order to be able to describe the process of transformation more precisely the Dewey-inspired concept 'operative ideational tools' is introduced. The concept 'operative ideational tools' is elaborated upon Dewey's and Gadamer's concepts of respectively 'ideas as plans of operation' and 'application' (see chapter 4) and 'judgement' as connected with interpretation and understanding. The concept 'operative ideational tools' will be presented and discussed in the paragraph 'the process of inquiry'. The idea is that in order to transform a problematic situation into a coherent whole there is a need of problem definition which is done by application of operative ideational tools. In this article the ingredients of this process is to be analysed and discussed in relation to the internship situation which, inspired by a metaphor used by Donald Schön, in contrast to the educational institution might be seen as a swampy lowland. Furthermore the process of mediation between being a student and a professional will be discussed with regard to the issue of learning to get hold of problematic situations in the swampy lowland and the educational context respectively.

The swampy lowland

An internship is a learning environment where mediation between being a student and being a professional is going on. When a student is on an internship she is situated in an environment where professional practice goes on. Schön described professional practice as a varied topography where a high ground and a swampy lowland respectively are present (Schön, 1983, p. 42; Schön, 1987, p. 3). The high ground is the place where problems are solved by application of research based theory and techniques. The interesting thing is that the problems on the high ground, according to Schön, very often are inferior and uninteresting problems. On the contrary, the problems in the swampy lowland, which is Schön's description of the messy area of practice, would be of greater interest for society to have solved. If it is assumed that the high ground has resemblance to what goes on in an educational setting it is predominately the swampy lowland that is the new challenge for the student.

On the internship, the idea is that the student is to mediate between being able to solve problems by research based theory and technique and to be a competent problem solver in the swampy lowland. What was learned in the educational setting is to be applied in a context where influencing factors such as organisational issues, deadlines, other employees and customers with specific needs and demands are present.

Coping with problems is on the one hand to identify and describe the problem and on the other hand to try to solve the problem. In order to develop possible solutions the student has to analyse and define the problems in the problematic situation she is facing. This process will, in this context be discussed by application of the concept of inquiry. John Dewey defined the concept of inquiry in the following way:

"Inquiry is the controlled or directed transformation of an indeterminate situation into one that is so determinate in its constituent distinctions and relations as to convert the elements of the original situation into a unified whole" (Dewey, 1991, p. 108).

Furthermore, Dewey described 'thinking' by use of the concept of inquiry in the following way: "simply the ways in which men at a given time carry on their inquiries" (Dewey, 1991, p.107). According to Dewey 'thinking' must be associated with action and practice. To think is not something which goes on in isolation in the human mind but is integrated in action.

Dewey's definition of inquiry will be applied to discuss what kind of learning environment an internship might offer and how the student is to mediate between being a student and a professional when coping with problematic situations. Mediation between being a student and a professional is on the one hand to be able to transfer learning from an educational context to a professional context, while on the other hand it concerns the student's understanding and performance of the role as a student on an internship.

The issue which is to be discussed is how the student learns by converting situations in the swampy lowland into coherent wholes and what it actually means to convert situations into coherent wholes.

The process of inquiry

In the university setting students write assignments and conduct projects in order to learn and to document that they are able to find their way in a disciplinary area. The process they are going through might, inspired by Dewey's definition of inquiry, be described as follows: The student is in an uncertain situation due to a struggle with defining the topic, the problem and the method. In this process the student tries to transform the situation into a unified whole where 'whole' is to be understood as a structure where relations between elements in the situation are identifiable and clear.

But what does it mean to transform an uncertain or un-determinate situation into a coherent whole?

An example might serve as a starting point for the discussion. In chapter one of this book, there is a case concerning the organisational learning student Susanne who in her internship had the challenge of solving tensions between two groups of employees in the company - the plant group and the consumer service group. The challenge was to involve employees from the plant group in the visiting programmes of consumer service. This is an example of an uncertain and un-determinate situation which the student Susanne is facing and which she is supposed to be able to cope with and to learn from. The example reveals that Susanne conducted interviews and joined meetings with both groups and that the result was very positive due to the mutual understanding that was achieved. But is it the case that Susanne transformed an un-determinate situation into a coherent whole or what did she actually do?

Dewey said in *How we think* that "There is not at first a situation *and* a problem" (Dewey, 2008, p. 201). What is going on is more complex due to the uncertain situation. In order to get hold of the situation the person who is facing the problematic situation metaphorically climbs a tree in order to get a viewpoint of 'how facts stand related to one another' (Dewey, 2008, p. 122). Dewey described this as determining relating structures, which implies that the student is to find a kind of pattern which gives meaningfulness to the situation. Dewey's analysis of getting hold of an uncertain situation has some likeness with Gadamer's hermeneutical way of thinking. The hermeneutical version of what Dewey called an uncertain situation might be 'the hermeneutic situation' (Gadamer, 1994, p. 301). Hermeneutic situations are characterised by being situations where the person involved does not have a full overview of the situation due to the fact that the person is situated in the situation. At the same time the person who is in the hermeneutic situation will be embedded in a horizon of meaning which on the one hand limits the persons understanding and on the other hand gives a direction to possible actions. Another useful concept from the phenomenological and hermeneutical tradition, which, is to be linked with the pragmatic ideas of Dewey is the idea of intentionality which is used to describe human beings as always being acting beings with intentions. This is an idea which Dewey certainly would agree with and which is implicitly expressed in his non-dualistic view on man. A consequence is that man is to be understood as a being which intentionally applies operative ideas to situations in terms of for example conducting a specific competence, which is based on ideas developed within a disciplinary area. The idea of seeing human beings as applying beings is inspired by

Gadamer and Dewey and combines the phenomenological and hermeneutical idea of intentionality, Gadamer's concept of application (Gadamer, 1994, p. 334) and Dewey's idea of understanding ideas, concepts etc. as a kind of tools in terms of being 'plans of operation':

"Ideas that are plans of operations to be performed are integral factors in actions which change the face of the world. Idealistic philosophies have not been wrong in attaching vast importance and power to ideas. But in isolating their function and their test from action, they failed to grasp the point and place where ideas have a constructive office. A genuine idealism and one compatible with science will emerge as soon as philosophy accepts the teaching of science that ideas are statements not of what is or has been but of acts to be performed. For then mankind will learn that, intellectually (that is, save for the aesthetic enjoyment they afford, which is of course a true value), ideas are worthless except for when they pass into actions which rearrange and reconstruct in some way, be it little or large, the world in which we live" (Dewey, 1929/1990, p. 111).

Human beings apply ideas to situations and ideas are implemented as competences, rules, attitudes etc. To be able to act the person has to link application, understanding and interpretation of the situation (Gadamer, 1994, p. 308) and to act by applying ideational operative tools. Gadamer's concept of the hermeneutic situation is to be understood in another theoretical framework than Dewey's concept of the uncertain situation, due to being concepts referring to different traditions, but both concepts give a perspective on what it means to be in a situation which is not yet understood and how the student is expected to act and to apply tools in order to make something happen. If the concepts 'wholeness', 'uncertain situation', 'hermeneutic situation' and 'application' on a meta-level are seen as ideational tools which might help an understanding of what the student is meant to do if she faces a problematic situation in her internship, the concepts offer the following overview: The idea of the hermeneutic situation offers on the one hand an understanding of what it is like to be a human being in the world. On the other hand it offers an understanding of what it means to be a student who faces a problematic situation in her internship. To be in a hermeneutic situation means that the person needs to combine interpretation, understanding and application in order to cope with the situation. In addition the whole situation is loaded with significance due to the idea that the student is embedded in what Gadamer defined as a horizon of meaning. The challenge for the student is to transform the situation into a kind of wholeness where plans for application of 'operative ideational tools' is to fit to the situation. The concept 'operative ideational tools' is developed as an elaboration of Gadamer's and Dewey's concepts of respectively 'ideas as plans of operation' and 'application' and 'judgement' as connected with interpretation and understanding. By applying ideas in terms of operative ideational tools the situation is hopefully transformed into a meaningful situation by connecting and linking elements of the situation into a coherent whole. In the process of getting hold of the situation the student is to choose among operative ideational tools in terms of concepts, models, laws, rules etc. and eventually to develop proper tools herself. To transform a situation into a coherent whole might be associated with Dewey's concept of intelligent action. Dewey used the concept 'intelligent action' to overcome a dualistic understanding of man. The concept of intelligence was applied by Dewey to understand rationality in an action perspective. For Dewey rationality concerns the ability to act in an intelligent way in situations (Dewey, 1990, p. 170; Biesta & Burbules, 2003, p. 22). Intelligent action involves analysis of the situation and reflection on the situation. To act intelligent means that the person in the situation conducts a kind of analysis and reflection, which is to be associated with judgement: "Intelligence on the other hand is associated with judgement" (Dewey, 1990, p. 170). Intelligence and inquiry are related concepts and both of them are relevant for the student who faces an uncertain situation. The student has to learn to analyse the situation, reflect on the situation and to make a judgement of what the best action might be. If the student succeeds the action might be called an intelligent action. In order to become a professional the student must learn to act in an intelligent way in line with Dewey's definition of the concept.

Mediation between the educational and professional practice

Schön, who is inspired by Dewey, discussed the difference between problem solving and problem setting (Schön, 1983, p. 40). The term 'problem solving' indicates that the problem is defined and what is left is to find the relevant tools and methods in order to solve the problem. This would be a way of thinking which is to be defined as technical rationality (Schön, p. 39) which according to Schön does not give an appropriate picture of problematic situations. In the professional practice problems do not present themselves as well defined (Schön p.40). Therefore the student on an internship is to learn to define the problem before trying to find a solution to the indeterminate or problematic situation. In an educational setting case studies and problem based learning are examples of teaching and learning strategies which are meant to imitate learning in professional practice and where the student learns to define problems and not just to solve readymade problems. To be able to formulate and define a problem in a professional practice is the challenge for the student. Dewey's concept of inquiry as converting an un-determinate situation into a coherent whole is a very good description of what it means to define a problem but the term 'unified or coherent whole' is not unproblematic and therefore it is to be discussed.

In Dewey's definition of inquiry, inquiry, according to Schön, is to be understood as intermediate and the instrumentality in converting the situation into a coherent whole is seen as a means to further action (Newman, 1999, p. 16). Dewey distinguished between 'affirmation' and 'assertion' in order to describe different types of judgement where the term affirmation is used for judgements, which are means to further actions while assertion terms are meant to be final judgements. (Dewey, 1991, p. 123). Due to the pragmatic view of Dewey he would prefer judgements to be intermediate.

In order to transform an indeterminate situation into a coherent whole operative ideational tools are needed. The student's condition is to be in a hermeneutic situation and in addition the student might be in an un-determinate situation. It means that the student is to rely on two kinds of wholeness: On the one hand the student is situated in a hermeneutic situation which is to be seen as a 'horizon of meaning-wholeness' and on the other hand, following Dewey's definition of inquiry, the student is expected to transform an un-determinate situation into a coherent whole.

The analytic strength of Dewey's concept of 'a coherent whole' in relationship to analysing the learning environment of the student on an internship is the concept's usability to put a light on the learning processes the student must go through. The student must get hold of the situation and during this process the student must choose and apply operative ideational tools to the situation. But how does the student know what kind of operative ideational tools which are the best ones and what are the criteria of 'a coherent whole'. A problem might be that there might be several ways of defining and solving a problem. In a research based educational context an important demand is that the student is able to explain every step in the process coming from an indeterminate situation to a coherent whole. This is a demand in the documentation of research processes and a demand of assignments and projects. But is it also a demand in a professional practice? It might not always be the case. The customer is happy if the product works and does not necessary need an explanation of how and why it is the case. The student in the internship is happy if the machine or the process of communication works and might think that this was it. In addition the student might think that in real work it is all about pragmatic solutions and 'theory' is not that interesting. The supervisor of the educational institution will have another opinion. The difference between a research situation and a practice context might be the difference between understanding and changing. Schön said:

'The practice context is different from the research context in several important ways, all of which have to do with the relationship between changing things and understanding them. The practitioner has an interest in transforming the situation from what it is to something he likes better. He also has an interest in understanding the situation, but it is in the service of his interest of change' (Schön, 1987, p. 72).

As it appears there might be a dilemma for the student. In the professional practice/the internship the aim is to change things while in the educational setting the aim is to understand things. But is it really the case? Is there necessarily a gap between being in a professional practice and an educational setting? The possible dilemma is to be seen from the perspective of Dewey's idea of transforming an un-determinate situation into a coherent whole. If the student in the internship understands the process of transforming an un-determinate situation into 'a coherent whole' as a process very similar to a research process the student will learn that the best practice would be the practice where she is aware of the operative ideational tools she is applying. Furthermore the student must be aware of the characteristic of the coherent whole she has created and in addition be aware that all coherent wholes might be challenged. That is, all coherent wholes are to be intermediate due to being constructed by human beings. The way a coherent whole is interpreted and constructed and elements identified in the whole might change into another picture with other elements. A point here is that it is not possible that everything in the process is fully transparent. Human action and thinking is not fully transparent for the actor. The process of interpreting, understanding and application might be understood as transactional (Dewey & Bentley, 1989, p. 101). Despite the messiness in transactional processes it is possible to discuss and document processes of change by clarifying how an indeterminate situation was transformed into a coherent whole and how plans for operation were designed and afterwards to analyse and learn from the process. If the student and the university teachers acknowledge the idea of inquiry as a process where an indeterminate situation is transformed into a coherent whole there might be a possibility of a better mediation between the educational and the professional practice. To be stressed is that the idea of a coherent whole is to be understood as a kind of operative ideational tool, which might help the student to clarify the process while coping with an un-determinate situation. The idea of a coherent whole might help the student to describe operative ideational tools applied in the process and to be aware of how these tools transform the un-determinate situation into a coherent whole. Furthermore, it might be that the student faces difficulties with transforming the situation into a coherent whole due to problems with available operative ideational tools. This problematic situation might help the student to be aware that both operative ideational tools and coherent wholes are to be challenged.

In the educational setting and especially in a PBL university such as Aalborg University the students are trained to cope with problems, which resemble professional problems (see chapter 8).

One difference between being in an educational context and in a workplace context is that problematic situations in the internship are not necessary meant and designed for learning. That is, the student is to find her way in the swampy lowland. A problem might be what a customer or the workplace wants handled.

What does the student learn by coping with these 'real' problems and what kind of learning environment is an internship? The answer must be that the student learns to convert a 'real-world' problem into a whole in terms of Dewey's definition of wholeness. The challenge for the student is to find her way between pragmatic solutions and solutions which are explicitly supported by research.

When the student is in the internship she has a position where she has to mediate between being a student and a professional. She is invited into the swampy lowland and she needs to find her position and role in the landscape. To find a position in this temporal work situation and to establish a kind of self-understanding as a professional is part of the learning challenge. The student is to learn and demonstrate that she is able to cope with un-determinate situations in the swampy lowland. At the same time the student must meet the demand of the educational institution which means that she must be able to account for operative ideational tools which are applied in the process and to characterise indeterminate coherent wholes which are constructed in the process of defining and solving problems.

Concluding remark

The aim of this article was to discuss what kind of learning processes an internship might offer when it comes to the student's ability to get hold of a problematic situation. To describe the process the concept of inquiry was applied. The challenge for the student on an internship is to mediate between being in an educational setting and a professional practice. Apparently the situations the student meets in the swampy lowland are different from the problematic situations the student meets in the educational setting. Another question is if the demands of the process of inquiry in an educational and a professional context should be different due to a 'change orientation in the professional practice and an 'understanding orientation' in the educational context. The answer must be that although problematic situations appear differently and the contexts are different the demands of the process of inquiry must be the same if the student is to learn from her visit in the swampy lowland.

References

Biesta, Gert J.J. & Burbules, Nicholas C., 2003. *Pragmatism and Educational Research*. Lanhan, Boulder, New York, Toronto, Oxford. Rowman & Littlefield Publichers Inc.

Dewey, John, 2008. *How We Think (revised edition)*. In: Boydston, A. (Ed.). *John Dewey The Later Works*. Volume 8. Carbondale and Edwardsville. Southern Illionois University Press.

Dewey, John, 1997. *Democracy and Education*. New York. The Free Press.

Dewey Press, John, 1990 [1929]. *The Quest for Certainty*. In: *John Dewey, The Later Works*. Vol. 4. Ed. by Jo Ann Boydston. Carbondale and Edwardsville. Southern Illinois University.

Dewey, John, 1991. *Inquiry*. In: Boydston, A. (Ed.). *John Dewey The Later Works*. Volume 12. Carbondale and Edwardsville. Southern Illionois University Press.

Dewey, John & Bentley, A.F., 1989. *Knowing and the Known*. I: Boydston, A. (Ed.). *John Dewey The Later Works*. Volume 16. Carbondale and Edwardsville. Southern Illionois University Press.

Gadamer, Hans-Georg, 1994. *Truth and Method*. New York. The Continuum Publishing Company.

Newmann, Stephen, 1999. *Philosophy and Teacher Education, A Reinterpretation of Donald A.Schön's Epistemology of Reflective Practice*. Aldershot. Ashgate.

Schön, Donald A., 1983. *The Reflective Practitioner*. USA. Basic Books Inc.

Schön, Donald A., 1987. *Educating the Reflective Practitioner*. San Francisco. Jossey-Bass Publishers.

Lars Bo Henriksen
Johan Askehave

Engineering students in the real world - on-campus PBL

The traditional lecture based teaching model, which is most often seen as *the* model for higher education, has its obvious limitations and problems. It is unable to establish interdisciplinary study programmes; it is unable to solve the problem of applying the knowledge gained to real life situations and in most cases there are usually problems of motivation.

PBL – problem and practice based learning has often been proposed as a solution to these problems (Kjærsdam & Enemark 1994; Kolmos, Fink and Krogh 2004; Kolmos & De Graff 2006). Aalborg University has a history of using PBL in most study programmes and the positive results speak for themselves. The students learn a lot and are very successful in the labour market after their graduation. On top of that the PBL structure ensures that the students finish their studies within the time scheduled in the study programmes and the PBL structure has been able to minimise dropout rates. The basis of the Aalborg PBL model is project work in student work groups. Each semester the students form groups of 3 to 8 students and each group work on a project where they analyse a problem within the field of study.

Recently the Aalborg University management have created a set of "Standards of Certification" (Aalborg University 2010) that form a set of guidelines for the Aalborg model. The reason for these standards was to establish a common ground for future debates on the PBL-model as well as assisting study boards in the on-going accreditation processes.

This chapter analyses the Aalborg PBL model. Why is it apparently so successful, what does it do to the students and what are the possible pitfalls that should be avoided when using PBL as a pedagogical model? The analyses are based on the description of the Aalborg Model as described in the "Standards of Certification" and on a case study of a group of students working on a project under the engineering study programme in environmental management.

The Aalborg model

The Aalborg Model has proved its worth. The candidates learn a lot, they graduate within the time scheduled in the study programmes, they get jobs and they earn more than candidates from other universities (Villesen, 2010).

In a draft proposal dated June 2010 the rector and pro-rector of Aalborg University together with PhD fellow Scott Barge suggests nine principles for PBL certification:

"The aim of this document is to capture the essential components and ideals of the Aalborg PBL model. Thus the *Principles of Problem and Project Based Learning* may be used to introduce new students, new members of staff, external constituents, etc. to the educational vision that shapes what Aalborg University does and what the university hopes to achieve."

The principles consist of nine points:

Educational vision. That is, an educational institution that wants to adopt a PBL approach "has an agreed upon and clearly articulated vision for how problem and project based pedagogies are integrated into its institutional objectives".

This point also clearly describes the content of the Aalborg PBL model:

A. Problem orientation; the students work on problems of their own choice within the chosen discipline.
B. Project organisation; each semester the students work on a problem in a project.
C. Integration of theory and practice.
D. Participant direction.
E. Team based approach. That is the students work on their projects in groups.

In all, all parties involved at the university and its educations should be committed to the support of the PBL model.

Curriculum. The PBL model should be written into all curricula and the project work should comprise at least fifty percent of all academic credits.

Assessment of students. All students are assessed on the basis of the PBL principles.

Faculty. Faculty members should demonstrate a clear understanding of the PBL model. All faculty members should be introduced to PBL.

Students. Students should demonstrate knowledge of and commitment to PBL. This also ensures that the students learn project management through their projects. Thereby the students will actively keep the learning process going.

Resources. The university should provide students and faculty members with the recourses necessary. This includes group rooms, library facilities, computers etc.

In addition to these six criteria the "Standards of Certification" mentions three additional points, which are **programme administration**, **external relations** and **educational research** which are all seen as necessary parts of a successful PBL programme.

The principles of PBL as described above is an ideal type PBL model and it could be seen as a rough sketch of what is going on in most study programmes at Aalborg University. If the model is as successful as suggested – and there are good reasons to think so - the question is what it does to the students, or rather how do the students use the PBL model to learn? In the following we shall analyse a group of students using the model. The students learned a lot and they were very satisfied with their results.

The case – engineering students, on-campus practical learning

The study programme "Urban, energy and environmental planning" is an interdisciplinary programme based on both engineering and social science, aiming at a master's degree in engineering. The education is concerned with urban development, energy and environment in local and international contexts.

This case concerns a group of first year students and their second semester project. The overall theme of the second semester is 'Urban ecology planning'. The focus of the theme is how to integrate urban ecology into the planning of a new or existing urban area, district or a specific construction. According to the study programme the purpose of the second semester project is to "...enable the students, in a methodical way, to carry out the problem-based and project-organised form of learning in groups, with belonging evaluations of the achieved results and a total conclusion...".

The product
Group B332 (the number on the door to the group room) worked on a project dealing with torrential rain on a suburban street. The climate of the earth is changing and the consequences are visible already today: The global average temperature has increased by approximately 0,8 degrees Celsius since 1850, and as a result of that an increase in torrential rainfall will be seen in Denmark. That is the reason why group B332 investigates how to handle extreme rain on a suburban street in their report. The group has chosen an actual street in Aalborg called Davids Allé as their case.

The Municipal District of Aalborg has decided to install a new dual drainage system in the entire city a.o. to prevent inundations/floods in the event of torrential rainfall. Davids Allé has already installed the new dual drainage system and the project developed by group B332 investigates how the new drainage system can be further supplemented in situations where the drains cannot handle the massive water volumes of torrential rainfall.

The written report that was the end product of the project work identified which drainage system would be technically feasible to implement on Davids Allé. Furthermore, the report investigates the environmental advantages and disadvantages of the different systems plus the social aspects of these systems.

The report concludes that the amount of water that falls during torrential rainfall cannot be successfully absorbed by the new dual drainage system alone. However, by implementing the solutions suggested by the project group, Davids Allé can be protected from flooding during future torrential rainfall.

The project
After the study programme had been handed out, group B332 started discussing what the project should be concerned with, what topic to choose. The study programme gave them a framework, some guidelines, and it was within these guidelines that they had to decide the topic of their project. The group already knew that the project had to deal with urban ecology in some way and they quickly decided to

work with climate change and climate adaptation; more specifically, increased precipitation. Within adaptation of increased precipitation there are many interesting problems. But based on the common interests of the group and their dialogue with their supervisor, group B332 chose to focus on ways to handle increased torrential rain on a suburban street.

The next step was to make a problem-analysis. By making the problem-analysis the group achieved new knowledge - knowledge which primarily came from secondary data sources such as articles and reports. The group also interviewed an expert in order to get more specific knowledge about certain issues within the problem-analysis.

After writing the problem-analysis the group had enough knowledge about the issue of increased torrential rain on a suburban street, so that they were able to come up with a lot of interesting questions, which led to the problem statement. With the problem statement in place, group B332 spend some time discussing what kind of knowledge and data they had to collect in order to answer the problem statement. Once again the supervisor of the group was consulted. She helped the group with some of the data collection, and advised the group on how to do interviews.

Once the data was collected the group were ready to perform the analyses necessary in order to answer the problem statement. In the analyses different methodologies were used; such as interviews, geographic information systems and a literature survey. Now the group were able to answer the problem statement.

The process

The study programme set up some goals for the second semester project. These goals were obviously included in the goals which group B332 had for the project-process. Furthermore, the group aimed towards producing a project with high professional standards as well as building on their experiences from the first semester project.

Each member of the group had their own goals and expectations of each other and of the group itself. After the formation of the group, the members discussed these goals and expectations, and the results of these discussions were written down along with the expectations of the supervisor together with the project's criteria for success as defined by the group. The goals and criteria for success were that everyone should do their best and take responsibility. The working relationships of the group should result in a report that every member of the group could vouch for. Honesty was weighted high along with the fact that everyone should contribute with their opinions and point of views. Furthermore, it was important that the group would create a good working environment because it motivates and creates a better atmosphere within the group as well as the fact, that it is often easier to give and take constructive criticism once people know each other well.

In the start-up phase of the project the group found it important to collect as much knowledge about the subject as possible. Therefore, each member started reading about the subject. Group B332 discovered that this phase was not structured very well. Nobody really knew who was reading what, which meant that one member of the group could be searching for information about a topic when one of the other group members already had the necessary information. At a later stage knowledge-sharing worked well for the group. They succeeded in exchanging and reading each other's notes with the result that everybody knew and understood the things the other members of the group were writing about.

Group B332 had a common goal about achieving new qualifications during the process of the project. That also involved planning and management. The group aimed at making the process as clear and structured as possible, so the risk of losing the general picture would be reduced. Therefore the group made a timetable that highlighted important dates, meetings, milestones and personal appointments throughout the process. Unfortunately it did not function as intended due to the lack of information that was written into the timetable. It meant that the group sometimes lost track of the process, and therefore the group, for some time, did not proceed as planned. But five weeks before the final deadline, the group saw the necessity for a properly functioning timetable. In this timetable, the group wrote down which chapters needed to be produced, when a sketch of the chapter had to be made and when the chapter had to be completely finished. At first sight the group thought the plan was a bit confusing, but still everyone saw the necessity of having and following the plan. It turned out that the new timetable worked very well. The group thought that it became a lot easier to see which chapters needed reworking and to delegate the work of the various chapters among the members. The last five weeks before the deadline the group had to work hard in order to follow the plan, but they succeeded and as a result of that, they were able to finish the project in time without too much stress.

Group B332 chose to spend most of the time working with the project in the group room on campus. They would typically meet around 8.15

am and go home by 4.00 pm. The group would start the mornings by summing up the work from the day before and discussing what needed to be done. In the second half of the project process, the group began using the boards in the group room. Things that had to be done or needed a little more work were written down on the boards, which meant that everybody knew what to work on at all times. Not every member of the group had tried this working method before. It meant that for some members of the group, it required some adjustments. The benefits of working together on campus were obvious; everybody had a common understanding of the direction of the project, and it kept the group on track from the beginning right to the end. Another advantage was that when they worked for eight hours on campus they did not expect each other to work on the project after 4 pm. It meant that the members of the group did not have to think about the project in their spare time, which prevented the group from breaking down.

The group consisted of six students, which is a relatively large group. When working in large groups, it is hard to completely prevent conflicts and tensions from happening between the members. Group B332 was no exception; sometimes there was a tendency for some group members to say things a little too directly, which other group members were not used to and therefore these types of remarks could be regarded as offensive. But in general the members of the group were good at not bearing any grudges, which of course is a great advantage because it meant that there would be no tensions the rest of the day if there had been a discussion earlier on. The group members learned to address criticism towards the project instead of the person.

Due to the size of the group, there were many different opinions during group discussions. Group B332 considered this a good thing, as it gives one a wider and more varied look at the subject. Sometimes it meant, that the group would spend a lot of time discussing, and sometimes found themselves discussing the same things over and over again. To avoid this problem and become more efficient, group B332 talked about writing down the results of the discussions, so the time could be used in the most appropriate way.

Overall, the group considered their work relationship successful. Deadlines and schedules were kept, and if a member of the group had any problems meeting a deadline the person informed the rest of the group.

The group held several interviews during the project. Two of these interviews were with citizens in Davids Allé. The first interview was considered a success by the group. The second interview on the other hand, did not work out so well. The group erroneously developed the interview-guides the same way, even though they had to conduct two different interviews. The first interview dealt with a process, which the citizens had been through themselves and therefore focused on their background knowledge and opinions on the subject matter. In the second interview the citizens were asked to consider things, they had not been introduced to before, and therefore had no background knowledge of. The group had not discussed their expectations of the second interview, nor had they talked about how the results from the interview should be processed. This meant that the interview was not structured well enough and too much information was given to the citizens, which made them a bit confused and made it hard for them to make up their minds about the questions. From this experience, the group has learned to clarify the purpose of the interview and how the results should be processed before conducting the interview. Furthermore, a pilot study of the interview would have been useful in order to prevent the mistakes the group experienced during the second interview.

The decision-making process in the group did not always proceed without problems. The group often found themselves, during the beginning of the process, not being able to take decisions on their own. Instead, the group would lean towards their supervisor. This meant that the group would often discuss the same things twice. As the project work progressed the group became better at making decisions, and towards the end this was not a problem. The improvement happened partly because the group realised that is was a waste of time and partly because they became frustrated about it and therefore took action. For future projects the group has decided to write down important decisions that are made and in that way solve the problem.

Analysis - what does it do?

The project developed by group B332 is a case of an ideal type PBL learning. The case fulfils all requirements from the "Standards of Certification" of the Aalborg Model. At first glance a project about floods in a suburban street, drainage systems and the prevention of floods does not sound as the most exciting thing to be concerned with when you are a young engineer to be. But it turned out that the project was both interesting and exciting and it proved to be a very good opportunity to do something that engineering students could learn a lot from.

During the process of the project, group B332 has picked up a lot of experiences with project work and project management. Some of the most essential skills that the group have learned are the realisation of the importance of having a general overview of the project and the working process. In this project, the group decided relatively late the direction in which the project should go and it was only when there was five weeks of the working period remaining that they developed a specific timetable. In later projects group B332 will try to change this in order to always have an idea of what needs to be done plus the deadlines the need to be met and subsidiary goals to aim for. Furthermore, during the whole process the group want to have a general overview of who is doing what and how far people are with the various chapters. So, in this respect the group fulfilled the requirements laid out in the study programme. This was also evident in the final exam, where the group all got top marks for their project. Besides the skills in project management the students also learned how to conduct an interview, they learned how to calculate water flowing in a drainage system, they learned about floods and how to prevent floods. They learned about urban planning and the politics of planning and they learned how the overall study programme integrates engineering and social science. All this was based on the PBL project.

If we look at the project from the perspective of the principles of the Aalborg model we are able to see some of the reasons why the students found this project interesting and why they learned from the process.

Problem orientation. The project started out with a real life problem – the flooding of Davids Allé. The students analysed the problem and made a problem statement, found relevant methods and they solved the problem and found possible solutions to the problem of flooding. The semester was organised with this clear emphasis on the project organisation.

Integration of theory and practice. The project was a cross disciplinary project, combining engineering methods and methods from the social sciences. Because of the problem orientation the integration of theory and practice was part of the project already from the start. The students used models of water flowing in drainage pipes, but the way they learned this was not through lectures or any traditional teaching method. Instead the students saw that they needed these models and calculations in order to solve the problem. They needed to know how much water the present drainage system could handle and thereby finding the reason for the flooding. They found and asked people at the university who could give advice on which models to use and how to make the calculations and they had to teach each other how to use these models and calculations. This was not easy, but possibly far easier than learning it through lectures, where it would be difficult to see the reason for learning about these rather complex models. So, through the problem orientation and the integration of theory and practice the motivation for learning was definitely in place.

Participant direction. The necessity of learning about water flow is also a case of the participant direction build into the PBL-model. The general idea behind participant direction is that if the students are in the driver's seat and they themselves take charge of the project, they will learn more because they are the active part in the learning process. They are not passive receivers of something, but are actively seeking the knowledge they need in order to solve the problem and in that process of problem solving they learn. This was evident in the case of group B332. They conducted more than 14 interviews with the relevant actors concerned with the flooding of Davids Allé and they found these interviewees themselves on the basis of what they needed to know and who was available. As described above they made serious errors during some of these interviews and even if some of the interviews failed completely they were invaluable as a learning process.

Team based approach. The group used the team-based approach to organise their work. This meant that the team members made agreements on how to work. This is about motivation. Through the agreements the members made rules and regulations to be followed and this also meant that the students could use this as a kind of disciplining devise. That is, they could refer to the rules if anyone was not contributing to the project as agreed. The group soon learned that discipline was a vital and necessary part of the PBL setup and the group also learned that it is important to work hard and be dedicated to the group, because each student will get a reputation for either being someone who is hard working or someone who is not. This is important for the future projects, because those students who are not contributing to the project will find it difficult to be part of a group in the future. Rumours spread quickly at the university.

The students also learned how to handle disagreements between group members in a civilised manner and they learned the importance of project management – the case of the board clearly shows that. Peer learning became a vital element in the group's work as a learning process. The students would teach each other in the group room and in that way they ensure that all group members were on top of the problems they were working with.

To sum up; the students learned a lot because they took charge of their own learning. They made agreements that kept the project on track and disciplined the work of the group. They used peer learning and that way they made sure that every member of the group was well informed about the progress of the project work. They also spent a lot of time on their project and their studies in general. A recent survey showed that university students in Denmark on average spend twenty-five hours a week on their university studies. But the students in group B332 spent much more than that. They were on campus for what equals a normal workweek – between 35 and 40, depending on deadlines. In all there is every reason to see the PBL model as a very fine way of learning.

Conclusions

The Aalborg PBL model is perfect for providing engineering students with the competencies necessary for succeeding in today's labour market. Through the group work, the peer learning and the problem orientation the students acquire knowledge about engineering as well as about problem solving and project management. The integration of theory and practise ensures that the students can see the relevance of the different theories they meet during the semester which in turn secures the motivation for learning - in all a very successful model of teaching.

References

Aalborg University, 2010. *Standards of Certification - The Aalborg Model for Problem Based Learning*. Aalborg. Aalborg University.

Kjærsdam, Finn & Enemark, Stig, 1994. *The Aalborg experiment: Project innovation in University Education*. Aalborg. Aalborg University.

Kolmos, Anette, Fink, Flemming K. and Krogh, Lone (Eds.), 2004. *The Aalborg Model: Progress, Diversity and Challenges*. Aalborg. Aalborg University Press.

Kolmos, Anette & De Graff, Erik, 2006. *Management of Change – Implementation of Problem-Based and Project-Based Learning in Engineering*. Rotterdam. Sense Publishers.

Villesen, Kristian, 2010. *Kandidater fra de små universiteter tjener mest. (Graduates from the small universities earn the most)*. Information 090610.

Lone Krogh

The Aalborg PBL model and employability

Introduction

Labour markets have in many ways been undergoing many changes during the last number of decades. At the same time working life – whether in the private or public sector – is becoming ever more complex and unpredictable, technologically as well as in terms of qualifications, competencies, values and attitudes among employers and employees. The changes have had an impact on jobs, work functions, company structures as well as industrial dynamics. However, it has also had an important impact on the daily social life and the dynamics of the economy and society (Sennett, 2006). It has been explained as a change from the industrial society to the information society, the knowledge society, and even to the learning economy and society (Lundval, 2001). The changes are supposed to not only have an impact on society in general and on firms and institutions as such but they also affect relationships between people in all their mutual activities.

These tendencies influence the requirements for professional, general and personal competencies of academic staff. Relating to the professional foundation of disciplines within the individual subject and profession, we see a demand for abilities in development, planning, knowledge processing, theoretical reflecting and problem solving (Globalisation Council, 2006). Specific requirements to academics of course vary depending on the job being in upper secondary school, in public administration, consultancies or international private production companies, but general 'transferable' skills are in high demand at all academic work places. This of course demands changes in the functions of higher education institutions in order to be able to support students in developing skills and abilities as citizens, workers, and as adapters of new techniques, culture, and ethics of the future academic labour market.

Within universities it has become necessary to relate to education and teaching in a society and a labour market undergoing constant change. Referring to Bowden and Marton (1998), students must develop competencies designed for a society, which develops in yet unknown directions.

"The kind of learning we are interested in is learning which implies that the learners develop capabilities for seeing or experiencing situations or phenomena in certain ways.........Students can therefore be prepared for the unknown variation among situations in the future through experiencing variation in their education, which will enable them to discern critical aspects of novel situations" (Bowden and Marton, 1998, p. 24).

Consequently universities will be in focus, because they have an important significance in the diffusion of knowledge to society. Therefore the starting point for this discussion is the educational function particularly with a focus on its dissemination of knowledge to students besides the specific disciplinary knowledge. This focus is interesting because changes here can be important, but at the same time not undisputed as an obligation for universities. Generally, these kinds of changes are not, according to our experiences, the easiest messages of change to get accepted within the educational structures of universities. Further questions which will be raised and discussed in this chapter are how it is possible to secure the employability of students in an ever changing labour market and a changing society and how can we develop a complex combination of competencies structurally as well as methodically? In relation to this, the Aalborg PBL model will be discussed, taking results from large surveys into consideration, as a teaching and learning model with much potential.

Methodological approaches

The questions are addressed from data about the daily practice of 10.671 candidates and 364 employers in Danish and a number of foreign firms and institutions[1]. About 100 of the employers were interviewed also. At the same time parts of the same subject are addressed, for instance by the EU 2003 and in relation to the Bologna process (http://www.iu.dk/politiske-rammer/bologna-processen). Furthermore, questions are discussed in a number of more theoretically oriented writings within themes such as the new relationships between university and society, its part in the triple helix, (Dunne, 1999; Barnett, 1990; Wittrock, 1997; Eggins, 2003), the change from Modus One to Modus Two (Gibbons et al. 1994; Nowothy, 2001) in the production, and diffusion of new knowledge.

The importance of understanding the relationship between universities and society is connected to the social dynamics described within the concept of the knowledge or the learning society. All kinds of jobs and other social functions within this concept have to be dealt with more dynamically by individuals within a specific social context. Therefore substantial weight is put on buzzwords such as flexibility, dynamics, human resources, quality, skills for cooperation, individual and organisational learning. What does this mean to university education? Are the universities in fact not already providers of such demands and at the same time driven by a critical and autonomous pursuit for value free knowledge? In an ideal world driven by such a noble pursuit this could perhaps be the case. But it is different in a society increasingly marked by discontinuity, by changing politics and very different interests, and with universities, which are not able to fully meet the activities of value-free knowledge production. Due to these factors universities are increasingly forced to operate within a context of new management forms, new economic models, for instance marked by more research activities funded by external partners. At the same time universities have to be able to diffuse knowledge within the context of the so called mass university, which supports (as much as possible) even more diverse groups of students in developing the relevant academic skills and competencies in order to be able to participate in the academic labour markets of tomorrow.

In this respect, one may say that university education should not be totally market driven, as this might harm universities in one of their main functions as important correctives to societies. Furthermore the university would run the risk of educating an academic workforce with short-term competencies and skills, mostly concentrating on how to use skills already well known to the firms and institutions of today, and not on how to use genuine methodological skills for producing the knowledge of tomorrow. Therefore there are some skills and views on the production of knowledge coming from the production of disciplinary knowledge - and some more general university skills, which could be stored under the concept of "Bildung" (Bowden and Marton, 1998) that should counterbalance too much market orientation.

The perspective of the difficult balance, mentioned above, influences the discussions in this chapter, which affects the role of universities. The main empirical basis and inspiration are the messages given in the surveys with candidates and their employers. The candidates are those who are working within a Danish private and public sector context on the basis of the degrees they have acquired from the two Danish PBL universities (Aalborg University and Roskilde University).

Data from the surveys

The data contains information about how the candidates value the study they have gone through and how the knowledge and skills gained through the studies have helped them to get a job, and furthermore to progress them from a first job to subsequent jobs. The surveys also give us some information about how useful the knowledge and skills have been in their endeavour to understand the non-disciplinary requirements of the workplace, and how they have helped them to become professionals within their professional fields. Another theme, which is also an important element in the survey, is what the candidates would have preferred to have also gained from their university studies.

This is done to make the following analysis, which uses some of the data from the two surveys to focus particularly on *three themes*. *The first* is called job qualifications and is related to information on what is deemed necessary to manage a job as a candidate. *The second* is called preparing for a job and relates to information on what is needed to get a first job. *The third* is called the general academic qualifications and relates to information on non-disciplinary knowledge for future development of competencies.

The job qualifications

The most fitting way to see the needs for qualifications expressed by these candidates is to focus on the gap between what they find they have learned at the university and what has been expected from them at the workplace. This can be divided into skills – skills that are taught and learned and demanded skills. This could be described as: there are parts of the study programmes that the students find are very useful for them in a job situation, while other parts of the programmes were unnecessary, or missing from the programmes, relative to a future job situation. This information is of course based on the average of the entire sample and is covering a broad number of job functions in a large number of various firms and institutions and also a substantial number of study programmes with quite different scopes.

The skills, which are a balance between what the candidates value they have learned during their studies and what they found was needed on the job is for instance *the ability to acquire new knowledge*. In general, 98% of candidates within all areas found themselves well prepared to work project and problem-oriented, to analyse, to acquire new knowledge and have general methodological and theoretical subject related knowledge and to also work interdisciplinary. This may be deduced from the fact that some of the most important intentions of the two universities is to ensure that the students attending the educational programmes have the opportunity to develop those competencies. In the surveys, which contain data from the employers, it is expressed that the expectations they have is for the candidates to have abilities to work innovatively and project-oriented. Also, according to the data from the employers, the general theoretical subject related knowledge seems to be well matched between what was needed and what the candidates are actually able to handle.

Small differences were identified between acquired knowledge and needs within the specific subject area, but these differences were small and may be as a result of the dynamics in the development and change within specific knowledge areas. More substantial is the gap between the need for practical knowledge and business know-how within the field and the actual practical knowledge and experiences the candidates had before beginning their working life. From the surveys it is also evident that during the studies many students actually try to compensate for this by having practical training as part of their education i.e. part-time jobs besides their studies, and many of them write study projects in cooperation with firms and institutions. But still half of the candidates confirmed that such gaps do exist.

The biggest deficit seems to be communication and presentation competencies. A large majority of candidates stressed the need for such competencies, but only a few found that they had gained those competencies during their university studies. Here we are discussing areas that deal with rather personal competencies. The matter is also obvious when we discuss competencies related to the ability to work autonomously and under pressure. These aspects were also mentioned in the deficit list. Regarding competencies related more to the specific non-disciplinary skills area, was the ability to handle information technology where only the civil engineers expressed a balance while all other candidates expressed a clear deficit.

On the opposite side we also see gaps between competencies gained at the university and the competencies actually needed for the work. This is the case when we talk about general theoretical knowledge within the specific field or discipline and also on a number of methodological qualifications.

Preparation for an academic job

The surveys show that the study programmes lead to jobs in the ordinary academic labour market. The data, however, also shows that the time period between ending the candidates' study and getting the first job differs between the study programmes.

However, preparation for a job career has to be discussed within a framework of practical activities. One is the possibility to prepare for a job by writing the master thesis in cooperation with a specific firm or institution. Approximately 12% (2002) and 16% (2009) of candidates get their first job this way.

Another way of preparing for a job is to have a part-time job while studying, which is relevant to the area of study. There is an on-going debate on the pros and cons of students having part-time jobs while studying. In one corner we see some of those responsible for study affairs in several Danish universities and some Danish academic organisations[2] who recommend relevant work during the study period and extended study period. In the opposite corner we see the Danish government supported by some managers of study affairs, who are of the opinion that the students have to go through their studies within a limited study period therefore should not have a part-time job. What can be observed statistically from the surveys is that if the jobs are combined with some elements of practical training and cooperation with firms as part of the candidates' project work then the entrance to an academic job happens more quickly. The differences in the number of candidates who got a job within three months of having had such a job versus not having had one, however, was less than ten percent which was measured on the entire population. On the other hand the qualifications which are supposed to be gained through such activities seem to be valued positively not only by the candidates and some study managers, but also by the students. Therefore this might have to be taken into consideration in the discussion on non-disciplinary qualifications.

General academic competencies seen from the employer surveys

What is interesting from the employer survey is that they explain an increasing demand for university candidates in firms and institutions to have these kinds of general academic competencies. To the employers this increase will happen mainly because of an expected increase in the complexity of tasks and jobs in the labour market. This seems to be the dominating explanation of the employers for hiring Masters with additional competencies. At the same time the surveys show that the large majority (3/4) of employers' responses were that while the demands for disciplinary qualifications will remain unchanged in quantity, on the other hand the demands for non-disciplinary qualifications will probably grow in the future. This growing demand contains not only competencies such as the ability to network, to work across disciplinary borders, to change and to work in teams, but also the ability to understand the increasing political, social, economic and cultural interrelatedness within society.

The survey from 2009 shows that the employers generally find the employees well educated for the labour market. Six out of 10 firms give a high priority for "teamwork" as indicated by the following statements:

"Candidates from Aalborg University are incredibly well educated to work in teams." (A Human resource person from a big Danish IT firm).

A director from another IT firm says:

"... But what you specifically learn at university is difficult to tell somebody, for instance being able to build a radio or something similar. This is something you have to learn later on but you have found your way. What matters is the way in which you learn at Aalborg University. It makes up 80 % of the way in which we work. It is crucial because more than the exact knowledge has been put into their heads."

Conclusively the employers indicate the need for a future academic workforce with a complex combination of general academic (non-disciplinary) qualifications and specific disciplinary and professional knowledge. This raises the important question to which extent and how the universities have to meet these kinds of expectations from the labour markets. This will be discussed in the following section, taking some societal, economic, technological and cultural factors into consideration.

Demands for non-disciplinary knowledge on the job

As mentioned above in the employer's survey the employability of the candidates is related to social change, and the data can be seen as part of a general discourse on the future of the academic workforce. This future workforce contains, at least according to the EU commission (the Commission 2003), a number of characteristics based on how the demands for a university educated workforce develops. For the EU Commission this seems to be connected to the knowledge-based economy, to the need for interdisciplinary competence, for an ability to work globally in the local community, and to be able to manage a strategy of progression in the adaptation of new knowledge. These means are in EU terminology, elements in forming a strategy to increase the European competitiveness and according to the Commission ways to also solve more specific problems for European universities. This is done to see how they define the present and perhaps future society and economy and in this way perhaps make a perspective on the empirical data, and make a basis for changes needed in the universities.

One of the elements behind the changes can be defined as the technology factor. To some extent the universities have always been an important factor in the development of technology and university candidates have always been agents of technological and cultural change. This has been connected closely to the research within the disciplines and has defined not only the useful technologies, but also the way in which they should be used in an abstract form. In many professions we have seen a complete change in technology. What is also to be seen is a crossover of technologies between different professions. Examples can be health care technology and technologies for avoiding pollution.

These changes are both emphasising the need for being able to cross-disciplinary borders and they indicate the need for being able to reconfigure one's own knowledge. This is connected not only to the demand for being able to adapt to new knowledge after education, it also points in the direction of building up the capacity to do this both within formal and informal educational settings, cf. the Lifelong Learning strategy. This also connects to the expressed need for being able to participate in learning processes within the workplace and to some extent to have the ability to work or at least have some understanding on how to work within neighbouring fields. From a learning perspective this stresses the need for being able to participate in the production of new knowledge in the contexts surrounding the new techniques. This means to be able to participate in many forms of working and learning processes, not only continuing education, but also in learning opportunities, suddenly appearing in the network of customers, consultants, and experts in neighbouring fields. In addition to this the surveys show that for many of the candidates the direct participation in such processes is not enough - after a few years they are expected to be able to also lead such operations.

Connected to these changes in technology are a number of changes in expectations from the workplace, colleagues, clients, customers and management, which have been expressed by the employers of how a candidate should behave. From an old traditional concept of an academic workplace the young candidate started their career by working in a lower position within the Church, within the Courts or within the State administration and abilities to understand the hierarchy were preconditions for reaching higher positions. As the data from the surveys shows, today the great majority of the private firms and public institutions form a rather non-bureaucratic organisational setting both for the newly hired and for the more experienced employees. This kind of organisational setting demands a more proactive style of work for many occupied in the private as well as in the public sector.

This means that settling into the workplace in many ways has become complicated. As the surveys indicate, the candidates generally feel pressure to be able to perform for the employer and colleagues and to be able to practice within the profession from the first day of employment. At the same time the context for practising is increasingly unclear because the rate of change is growing and the organisational structure is more unstable. This can be a way to understand why many of the candidates urge the universities to increase the importance of the student–company cooperation during the education and also to increase the chances of them getting a relevant part-time job during their studies.

These activities are partly a way to train candidates to practice the discipline, but it also points in another direction that is also underlined in the survey. The candidates focus their efforts during their education to be able to work on developing their personal competencies. This is closely connected to handling the methods of the disciplines, but it also indicates the needs for competence to work innovatively, to act actively, to take responsibility for pushing the firm ahead, and even to be able to work as an entrepreneur. These areas represent the changing relationships between the individual candidate and the workplace and emphasises that employees with a candidate degree can no longer expect a work position where disciplinary theoretical skills are steered by a fixed job description in a stable organisational structure.

This is also a result of increased expectations from the employer, colleagues and the organisation or institution on the ability to cooperate. When a firm or an institution is no longer able to function as a fully-fledged bureaucracy with formal vertical communication channels, because this makes the organisation non-competitive, then the demand for horizontal coordination and cooperation increases. In the present dynamics this kind of cooperation cannot be regulated from the top of the organisation through directives, so it is much more in the hands of the individual employee and the small group of colleagues who cooperate daily to act within this kind of organisational structure.

Due to the fact that the candidates are supposed to participate in the development and diffusion of knowledge from the discipline also in cross-disciplinary settings they have to take a function where they actively, directly or indirectly, work at changing the work methods. This, however, also happens together with a workforce with a vocational, non-academic background. At the same time these changes have to obey the new rules, norms and culture within the organisation where the individual and personal competence concerning face-to-face communication, ability to work in groups, and to form groups around important change projects are key elements. When the surveys mention the ability to take responsibility and to cooperate actively this represents a perspective on the new organisational reality.

The present organisational structure and its values and culture are also increasingly exposing candidates toward the environment of their organisation. The old functions of many firms and institutions are under deconstruction (Normann, 2002). Therefore candidates increasingly become front line workers. This can be seen in the surveys for both the employers and the candidates as the need to be able to work across traditional borders, to be able to structure projects, to do problem-based work, and to be able to communicate and present ideas. Perhaps also the clearly defined need for being able to work under pressure can be seen as connected to this context. The skills for the candidates represented here can be summed up into the dynamic creative group worker, willing and able to take individual responsibility.

The surveys put the focus on skills and competencies at the workplace and connected to the job of the candidates. This is of course an important part of the interaction between disciplinary and non-disciplinary competencies and does form some kind of focus on the employability of graduates from universities. But from the perspective of the total human life: as citizens, as workers and as social beings some ideas of how such functions are interwoven could also shed some light on the long-term employability in society at large. To some extent the demands, expressed in the surveys, point in two opposing directions. One is to be ready for immediate workplace challenges. The second can be seen behind this, and it summarises competencies which are not only usable for work life, but also as general competencies as citizen and as social being – for life in the *Gemeinschaft* and in the *Gesellschaft*. The kinds of competencies for these activities are of a general educational nature or *Bildung*.

Universities meeting the new demands

Based on some of the results of the surveys we have to ask ourselves: How are the needs for changes met by the universities? This question can be divided into two. One is what the university ought to do; the other is what the university is actually able to do. This complexity has even to be supplemented by looking into the complex dynamics of the society, which tells us that what ought to be done and what can be done very much depends on what happens in the surroundings of the university, i.e. in the national and international society.

One way of looking at these questions is from the perspective of the *traditional academic position*. This perspective will state, that it is not for the universities to speculate on profane changes in society as long as the university education is based on the most advanced research and knowledge within the discipline. If firms, institutions and society in general do not understand how to benefit from it, then they have a problem – not the university. From this perspective the universities would concentrate solely on producing new knowledge within the traditional disciplinary paradigm and go for valid knowledge.

Not only for citizens and employees, but also for teachers and researchers, this position, which can be heard presented in situations of political turmoil around universities, seems to be irrelevant in today's integrated funding, goal defining and cooperative inter-relatedness between the universities and the political context it is living in. On the other hand it is clear that there has to be some kind of limit, which cannot and should not be crossed by the universities in the tasks they work with and the methods they use.

It is important to recognise that an organisation can never establish a steady position between a total autonomous position and a total submerged position in a society with strong technological, social and cultural dynamics. This means that what can be said about the task of the universities, diffusions of non-disciplinary knowledge, and the development of employability can only become a kind of path. To discuss the direction of this path some of the elements from the surveys can be used as markers.

The first marker is the role of the university to engage in producing and disseminating knowledge about specific technologies. This is not a question, which has a simple answer, because both the candidates and the employers would find it very practical if the candidates were "good to go" from the first day at work. In addition to this, many of the activities around the primary study activities, such as training periods and part-time jobs parallel to studies aim to prepare the candidates. But to make this a primary educational task for the university develops the risk that they become so vocationally oriented that the diffusion of general and abstract knowledge drowns in a large amount of disseminating activities on knowledge about specific technologies and how they should be used in specific firms. So this might be a dangerous strategy.

The second marker is how much responsibility the university has when it comes to creating employability through the training of students in understanding the function of workplaces, companies and institutions. As long as the university was the only supplier of workforce candidates to a limited number of functions within specific types of institutions, this monopolistic position gave the university, the knowledge of how things were shaped in those institutions. It also had some kind of upper hand in conducting those minor scale changes that happened due to the production of new knowledge within the trade or profession, because the knowledge was produced in the university.

During a number of years the universities have lost this position mostly because the workforce educated in the universities have themselves managed to become important producers of new knowledge outside the universities. Many research divisions in big companies are several times larger than most university departments within the same field. In addition to this many more development-oriented functions in large companies have simulated methods developed in university research and reshaped them to be used in the companies. Human resource management could serve as an example here.

In disciplines where the universities educate Masters to work in such kinds of systems and where the majority of candidates get a job within companies or institutions, like that the workplace practice and knowledge about company culture seem informally to become part of the common knowledge within the education. An important question here is to what extent the knowledge among teachers from their research cooperation with companies is diffused systematically into the educational programmes as part of research-based teaching. One of the consequences of the increased number of students and the increased economic efficiency has in many university departments resulted in a clearer separation between study programmes and research, which may be a problematic strategy.

The third marker can be how far university education can be stretched in the direction of training the students to become cooperative partners to colleagues in their future work life. In general this is not a common subject in university education except for education where a professional involvement with other people is a main part of the profession and where practice is regarded as a necessary part of the education. For a candidate in communication, in social work, psychology, medicine and perhaps in public administration such skills and competencies will be taught as a part of the study programmes. But from the data of the surveys there seems to be a general wish for improvement of the curriculum, which has a broader range. It can therefore become a theme also in engineering, business administration, and gradually in many other master programmes to create programmes for students to teach workforce competencies in order to be able to function in cooperation with professionals from other disciplines.

This path does not have to be followed very far before it becomes easy to imagine that such skills are needed within many professions. It relates to participating in informal learning in the workplace, to group transformation of theory into action, to all kinds of entrepreneurship, to working with tasks and technologies that cross disciplinary borders, and in general to be able to fit into a workplace and an organisation. However, this also reveals something about the complexity of the tasks and how much they relate to the social competencies of the individuals. This raises another problem of how these goals would be possible for students to reach in disciplines where neither the motivation of the students nor the skills of the teachers are always directed this way. The basic situation must be different between an educational programme in medicine and an educational programme in mathematics, as the fist has a well-defined curriculum concerning practical skill, while the latter have none.

The fourth marker can be seen as a kind of summary of the previous three because it relates to the general education or Bildung-perspective. The motivation for general academic knowledge has to be connected to the discipline, but it cannot be led from this perspective alone because this will make it too narrow and led too much from the paradigm(s) of the disciplines. This makes it very difficult to deal with, particularly in a situation where the battle at the universities to some extent is between Modus One (more traditional research) and Modus Two (knowledge production) (Gibbons et al. 1994). The Modus Two will define general knowledge as working with the applicability of the discipline in cross-disciplinary contexts.

To defend the case on improving the general academic knowledge we might gain some power from the idea of "universalis" as part of the obligation of the universities. Non-disciplinary elements do relate to general and cross-disciplinary areas. If these areas do not include training in critical thinking in the idea of innovative and knowledge expanding work, and in ways these elements are related to knowledge in general, society in general and also human interaction in general, the very idea of university seems to lose important parts of its reason. So therefore this perspective should not be lost.

Principles of problem oriented project work and its institutional settings

The empirical data concerns two universities using Problem Based Learning strategies. Therefore some of the important aspects of this university didactics will be discussed in the perspective of students developing general and social competencies integrated in the development of disciplinary knowledge. This will highlight some of the ways in which the universities can be inspired and learn from its environments, and how subjects can lead to an actual learning process for students.

It is important to stress here both the character of the learning institution that the candidates in the surveys have gone through and the working culture as it relates to the two specific universities with their distinct didactical principles. The two universities in Roskilde and Aalborg are both based on the ideas of experienced based learning, inspired by for instance Negt, (1975)and Dewey, (1991).

The didactics were developed from original principles formulated around principles such as: problem orientation and interdisciplinary, exemplarity, open curriculum and experience-based learning, peer learning and cooperative learning in groups, (Kolmos et al., 2004). The original idea and theoretical foundation of the problem oriented project work in a Danish context was formulated by Illeris (1974)[3].

Based on analysis of society's need for education Illeris lists three categories of qualifications which appear to be necessary for the development of society: 1) Skills which can be defined in direct relation to a given task or work process, 2) Adaptive qualifications of a general character and comprising attitudinal characteristics (e.g. diligence, perseverance, vigilance etc.) – combined with a willingness to apply these characteristics in relation to work, to accept and subject to the existing work processes, 3) Creative / innovative qualifications which may be divided into qualifications for scientific, innovative work and qualifications for continuous renewal and being able to cooperate (Illeris, 1974, p. 32). Referring to Piaget's theory of learning Illeris understands accommodative learning processes as the prerequisite for creativity.

The problem oriented project work was and is characterised by:

- *Problem orientation*. The point of departure is the subject related knowledge, methods and theories relevant to the specific problem. Interdisciplinary becomes a leading principle.
- *Participant direction*. Both the definition of the problem and the choice of work methods must lie with the students, as this is the only way to create the possibilities for accommodative learning processes necessary to develop creativity and flexibility.

Furthermore, the problem in question has to be and be experienced as relevant for the individual student in order to ensure the appropriate learning process.

As a consequence of this the principle of participation in decision-making becomes important.

- *The principle of exemplarity*. Working with the important and representative aspects exemplifies the area of the discipline in question.
- *Group work*. The students collaborate in groups about problem solving. In that way they learn the difficult art of collaboration and leaderships of projects.
- *The communicative didactic*, with primary focus on the forms of work and cooperation within the group and the considerations regarding the choice of content.

The PBL work at the two universities may be interpreted and implemented in a number of different ways according to different curricular frameworks, disciplines, and learning goals. There may be varying degrees of free choice regarding the specific problem, subject area, and method, and the project work may differ in size, i.e. the students' workload per semester. Furthermore, there may be vast differences in resources allocated to the project work in terms of hours of supervision as well as study rooms for the groups

The project work is closely combined with lectures, seminars or laboratory work on relevant subject matters. The students' work is facilitated by university teachers supervising their project work. It is generally expected that students work in groups. Individual project study is accepted, but the students are told that this minimises peer learning.

The didactic of the two universities has been developed from the original principles formulated around the principles mentioned above. This means that all the students in the survey have been educated through Bachelor and Candidate Programmes, which in different combinations are built on these principles. They work in projects on defining, analysing and solving theoretical as well as methodological and real world problems. Some projects are empirically based on and are carried through in cooperation with firms, institutions, NGOs or other types of organisations. The selection of a problem and the nature of the project are closely connected to for instance the type of educational programme, whether it is graduate or post-graduate programme, and under which theme it is defined.

The work process has some similarities to some types of research work, but it also relates to types of work processes in business particularly in project management and in combination with organisational learning. This kind of educational work makes it possible for the students to participate in defining the assignments they have to work on. In this context there are similarities to the principles of Modus Two research. Especially in the last terms of the Candidate Programme the students have possibilities for transcending barriers of cognitive and affective aspects. This is done by having the students work in investigating learning processes prior to the research processes. The intention is not to turn all students into researchers but that the students develop competencies, which are useful within their future professional work.

From the surveys some of these goals seem to be met according to the candidates and their employers. This can be said about the theoretical knowledge, the methodological knowledge and some ability to cross the traditional disciplinary borders. In this respect these pedagogical and didactical principles seem to meet some of the demands also outside and across the strict disciplinary knowledge, without losing the learning of relevant disciplinary knowledge – still from the perception of the employers and their employees.

This turns the perspective to those non-disciplinary elements, which are not met sufficiently in the pedagogical form the candidates have been going through. Important elements here are the deficits in building a capacity to communicate professionally and in using presentation techniques. Of course these are also important competencies as candidates are starting a new career within a public or private organisation. However, it raises the question, what are the main obligations of the universities, which can be expected within the educational areas? Is it possible to guarantee the development of narrow discipline related competencies as well as all kinds of non-discipline related competencies? The two Danish universities, which are referred to in this paper may to a certain extent benefit from the fact that the organisational structure, the culture and the educational traditions have been for many years based on principles, which actually make it possible to establish a dialogue with the environments.

This is used to inspire students to participate in the discovery of new knowledge and problems in relation to future work situations and within society and to permanently use the inspirations from candidates, employers and other interesting diffusers of knowledge. However, maybe these two universities also have to discuss whether there are other didactical methods, which might be useful in the creation of relevant academic disciplinary as well as non-disciplinary competencies to participate more effectively in the creation of "lifelong" learning processes. This could gradually meet some of the non-disciplinary demands necessary for supporting the more long-term employability.

In relation to this, the main questions have been addressed: How is it possible to secure the employability of students to an ever-changing labour market? How to develop a complex combination of competencies structurally as well as methodically? Knowledge and understanding are essential elements in such processes, - and so it has always been within institutions of higher education. Teachers in higher education want students to develop abilities such as understanding important concepts and their associated facts and procedures within the different subjects (Ramsden, 2003). At the same time they want the students to be able to think critically and to analyse different aspects of the problems they are working on. In his book Ramsden refers to different international surveys, which document this. No doubt the teaching methods and the ways in which the higher education institutions and the teachers understand the learning processes are important to be aware of when the university has to decide how to support the development of the relevant disciplinary and non-disciplinary competencies.

Policies and strategies for the university on creating employability

In general the surveys analysed in this chapter point out some areas where employability might be improved if elements outside subject or disciplinary knowledge play an increasing role in the curriculum of the universities. At the same time the two universities, Roskilde and Aalborg who defined the focus for these surveys, are both institutions that have built themselves a reputation for not looking too narrowly on what could be the educational role of the contemporary university. Therefore a number of these areas are at present covered by the educational policies of these universities. On the other hand many researchers and teachers at these two universities will stress the limitations to such policies of enlargement. Two points are important here: One is what the obligations are in this field for the universities, the other is how fit the universities are for taking up the new tasks.

From a traditional perspective, one of the main tasks for the university concerning the teaching part is to function as a kind of quality controller throughout exams. This control is primarily on the disciplinary qualifications of the graduating candidates. Viewed from a narrow perspective, employability was closely related to the ability to define the right competency.

It is still possible to meet a scholar of the old type, who underlines the traditional values of the autonomous university with no obligations other than to legitimate its old divine values. But the examples of Roskilde and Aalborg show, together with all other modern universities, that to a certain extent it is possible to meet with the criteria of employability. However, we do not think that all demands from students and employers should be met, because trying to fulfil one goal will often harm the fulfilment of another important goal, which has to do with other obligations for the university. Consequently it is important to avoid harming the obviously relevant disciplinary or subject related goals in order to fulfil non-disciplinary goals needed from the individual firms or students. This sounds in itself reasonable, but perhaps the surveys themselves already make such a statement less absolute.

What can be seen through the increasing dynamics within all disciplinary fields is a change from a more stable definition of the discipline and its main elements to a kind of unstable multi-centred structure where the content and borders of the disciplines become increasingly unclear. At the same time most disciplines include increasingly larger quantities of knowledge. The result of this might either be a kind of specialisation or a kind of abstraction in the understanding of the disciplines. Where the traditional educational institution aims at the specialisation, then the data from the surveys as well as the policies of the two universities show signs of increased abstraction, which try to cover the disciplinary dynamics through creating a more methodological and conceptual understanding. This is done through the project orientation, through the problem-based work, and sometimes through combining a number of different study activities under theoretically defined themes.

An abstracting process of that kind will take some non-disciplinary elements into its own context and work on the similarities between several disciplines. This may result in the characteristics presented in the surveys by the candidates on their education with its strong potential and at the same time to contain sufficient general academic knowledge, disciplinary knowledge and methodological skills at an abstract as well as on a more concrete level. What seems to be in shortage are a number of more practical skills, perhaps also practical disciplinary skills. Such skills might (with less difficulty) be taught and learned in a more specialised education, but they can be more difficult to be taken into a broad and methodological oriented education especially in relation to the growing diversity among the student population. So there seems to be the well-known trade-off between abstraction and specialisation also in these universities.

At the same time abstraction is not according to these educational principles to be reached as a kind of pure theory. What is presented for these candidates is a kind of practical abstraction defined as the ability to handle a complexity of problems by relating or even integrating theory into practice. The basic part of the problem-based learning is its ability to train students to work deeply in identifying and analysing complicated problems, to find solutions and even to propose solutions and possible actions. In this way they will often succeed in deep learning and reach the highest level in the SOLO[4] taxonomy (Biggs, 2007). Because of the complexity of many theoretical problems this offers no easy solutions. This means that the candidates, as they express, to some extent lack the abilities in finding the "quick and easy" solution. Competencies like that definitely have to be learned in the "real world" following the studies at the university

Challenges to the university

A main challenge is to be able to draw the border between what are relevant obligations for the university education and what is not. The challenge appears from the risk that university education becomes so oriented toward practice, the labour market, and non-university obligations that they forget their core tasks. The universities have to be aware of the importance of a certain balance between some kind of autonomous research and education.

These challenges can be summed up into the following viewpoints: *"..universities in many respects hold the key to the knowledge economy and society."* and *" ..Humboldt in his reform of the German university, which sets research at the heart of university activity and indeed makes it the basis of teaching,"* (The Commission, 2003, p. 5). Both these positions should be defended also in the future developments in university education under the prevailing precondition that *"..European universities generally have less to offer and lower financial resources than their equivalents in other developed countries,"* (The Commission, 2003, p. 3).

If the development of taking new elements of disciplinary and non-disciplinary employment aspects into the education is to be encouraged, it should be combined with other improvements. The educational structures should be able to improve its ability to handle the following elements: to remove all obsolete disciplinary parts of curriculum, to improve the pedagogical and didactical abilities of teachers, and to improve the students' ability as responsible learners. This is not only a challenge for more traditional universities, but also for universities using more "modern" didactical principles.

On the ability to remove the obsolete parts of the curriculum, the contemporary development within many disciplines becomes increasingly important, because the quantity of knowledge grows dramatically. At the same time it becomes increasingly difficult because the growth increases the multi-centeredness of many disciplines. This means that many non-disciplinary elements in the same process become integrated in the discipline, and so the definitions of disciplinary and non-disciplinary elements and what is the core of the discipline increasingly become a matter for dispute. To define this dispute as a legitimate part of the discipline in a way that it can be understood and worked with by students is perhaps the most important part of the didactical challenge. It is important to mention here that the concept of transparency has become an important aspect of all university education as a part of the Bologna process.

Improving the pedagogical ability of teachers does not have much to do with a standard pedagogical course. On the contrary pedagogical and didactical discussions need to be connected to discussions related to the improvement and changes related to disciplinary or non-disciplinary elements within individual studies. The most important thing here is to keep connections between research and teaching as close possible, and to use this relationship as the pivotal point for the different teaching activities. At the same time it is important to also look at the ways that non-disciplinary knowledge and knowledge from the "real world" is diffused to students. The knowledge coming from both sources are key elements in the students' adaptation of an academic and professional conceptualisation of the discipline.

This ends this exploration on the crucial point, the students who are important for developing a range of graduate attributes. If they are included as learners in the knowledge producing activities of the university they will be able to use the progression in disciplinary knowledge as inspiration for being responsible for their own learning processes. The university, however, has to be aware of how to ensure the students consciousness of these processes. If the students on the contrary are experiencing the university as some kind of "supermarket" where they are the customers, and where most of the merchandise is uninspiring and things seem to be a little too old fashioned then a large number of pedagogical techniques will not improve the students learning processes.

Therefore the surveys and the recommendations from the candidates and the employers have to create the basis for a discourse, which is not concentrating on the single elements of a non-disciplinary or non-subject character. Instead these recommendations should be used for a general disciplinary interaction between candidates, students and researchers/teachers on how the growing number of disciplinary and non-disciplinary elements can be assessed and used by the students during their studies at the university with the aim of improving their employability and their contributions to a dynamic society in the future.

Notes

1 The discussions in this paper are based on data from two surveys collected in 2002 from 6,758 candidates graduating from two Danish universities in 1992 to 2002 and from 175 employers; and in 2009 data from 3,913 bachelors and candidates graduating in 2003 to 2008 from one Danish university including data from 189 employers.
2 An investigation made by the Central Academic Organisation in 2010 shows the benefit of students having study relevant part-time jobs during the study period. http://www.ac.dk/files/pdf/Det_frie_valg_eller_det_frie_fald.pdf

3 The PBL model, implemented in Denmark was a result of needs for developing new more critical approaches to teaching systems.
   Theoretically the Danish PBL approach was originally based on ideas from the two German authors Negt and Kluge (1975) and with references to C. Wright Mill (1959), Dewey (1933) and Freire (1970).
4 **S**tructured **O**bserved **L**earning **O**utcome (Biggs & Tang, 2007).

References
Barnett, Ronald, 1994. *The Idea of Higher Education*. Buckingham. The Society for Research into Higher Education.
Biggs, John and Catherine Tang, 2007. *Teaching for Quality Learning at University*. The Society for Research into Higher Education. Maidenhead. Open University Press, McGraw-Hill Education.
Bologna declaration. *(http://www.iu.dk/politiske-rammer/bologna-processen.*
Bowden, John and Marton, Ference, 1998. *The University of Learning*. London. Kogan Page.
Dunne, Elisabeth, 1999. *The Learning Society*. London. Kogan Page.
Commission of the European communities, 2003. *The role of the universities in the Europe of knowledge*. Bruxelles. Communication from the Commission.
Dewey, John, 1991. *How we think*. New York. Prometheus Books.
Eggins Heather, 2003. *Globalisation and reform: necessary conjunctions in higher education*. In *Globalisation and Reform in Higher Education* (red. Heather Eggins). The Society for Research into Higher Education.
Freire, Paolo, 1970. *Cultural Action for Freedom*. Harmondsworth. Penguin.
Gibbons, Michael et.al., 1994. *The New Production of Knowledge. The Dynamics of Science and Research in Contemporary Societies*. London. Sage.
Globalisation Counsel, 2006. *Progress, Innovation and Cohesion Strategy for Denmark in the Global Economy – Key Initiatives*. The Prime Minister's office.
Illeris, Knud, 1974. *Problem orientation and participant direction. An introduction to alternative didactics*.
Kandidat og Aftagerundersøgelsen, 2002/03. *Roskilde Universitetscenter og Aalborg Universitet*. www.cand.aau.dk.
Kandidat og Aftagerundersøgelsen, 2009. *Aalborg Universitet*. www.cand.aau.dk.

Krogh, Lone and Gulddahl Rasmussen, Jørgen, 2003. *The contemporary and future criteria for employability for Masters and the university response. An analysis built on data from two Danish universities.* Paper for The Joint Air and EAIR seminar June 13–14, 2003 on Workforce Development and Higher Education.

Kjærsdam, Finn and Enemark, Stig, 1994. *The Aalborg Experiment. Project Innovation in University Education.* Aalborg: Aalborg University Press.

Kolmos, Anette, 1996. *Reflections on Project Work and Problem-Based Learning.* European Journal of Engeneering Education. Vol. 21 no. 2, p. 141-148.

Lundvall, Bengt-Åke & Archibugi, Daniele, 2001. *The Globalising Learning Economy.* New York. Oxford University Press.

Mill, C. Wright, 1959. *The Sociological Imagination.* Oxford. Oxford University Press.

Negt, Oskar, 1975. *Sociologisk fantasi og eksemplarisk indlæring (Sociological imagination and exemplary learning).* Roskilde University Press.

Normann, Richard, 2002. *Reframing Business. When the Map Changes the Landscape.* New York. John Wiley.

Nowothy, Helga et. al., 2001. *Rethinking Science.* London. Policy Press.

Ramsden, Paul, 2003. *Learning to Teach in Higher Education. 2nd Ed.* London. Routledge Falmer.

Sennett Richard, 2006. *Den nye kapitalismes kultur (The Culture of the New Capitalism).* Hovedland.

Wittrock, Bjørn, 1997. *Det moderne universitets forvandling. (The transformation of modern university).* In Rasmussen, Palle & Jacobsen, Arne. *Universiteter I dag. Politik - Kultur – Ledelse. (Universities today. Politics - Culture – Management).* Samfundslitteratur.

Pekka Kämäräinen
Ludger Deitmer

Lessons from the Euronet-PBL project

Introduction

In this chapter we summarise the main findings from the Euronet-PBL project. Firstly, we will present the Euronet-PBL project that has provided the basis for the findings. We take a look at the starting points, the approach and lessons learnt during the journey. Then we raise the question, what messages arise for wider discussion of practice and problem-based learning. The project was initiated to study and promote Practice-Based Learning in the emerging Europe Higher Education Area. The project has analysed practice-based learning arrangements as a specific form of university-enterprise cooperation and as an opportunity for self-organised learning. In this respect the project has chosen to study three academic domains – Business Administration, Engineering and Vocational Teacher Education. The initial assumption was that in these domains practice-based learning periods (*Praktika*) and placements (*Internships*) as well as company-oriented projects, have been considered as essential elements of the studies.

The partnership was based on six universities (research partners) from Germany, Norway, Turkey, Slovenia, Ireland and Denmark. Each research partner invited one or two partner enterprises and other associated partners (companies or professional associations) to join in the activities. In this way the project design tried to make local or regional partnerships obvious as essential preconditions for practice-based learning arrangements.

The empirical studies of the project were based on analyses of students' projects in different practice-based learning arrangements. In addition the research partners have produced stakeholder interviews with students, company representatives and with university lecturers. Based on the empirical analyses, the partners have organised local evaluation workshops that bring key actors, who have recently worked together, into a joint discussion.

The project has taken into consideration that the universities have followed different approaches to practice-based learning. Therefore, the arrangements are characterised by different degrees of involving students in real working life and different intensities of university-enterprise cooperation.

Participation of students in on-campus seminars with a focus on problem-based learning familiarises the students with company-specific problems without including actual participation in working life (see chapter 8 in this book).

Completion of individually arranged in-company internships (before the studies) or co-operative learning placements (during the studies) requires actual participation in working life but doesn't include intensive cooperation between university and enterprise.

Completion of curriculum-integrated practice-based learning periods (*Practicum*) in companies requires planning and implementation of workplace-related learning assignments from students. These arrangements require clear agreements between universities and enterprises.

Engagement of students in longer project-based learning cooperation with partner companies includes intensive participation of groups of students (for whom the project covers a major part of their studies). These arrangements require comprehensive cooperation agreements between the university and hosting enterprises.

In light of the above the project considered that diverse models are available, but there is no common quality of awareness. Therefore, the project sought to create a basis for a focused discussion on the benefits of the learning arrangements for the different parties involved.

The approach and the learning journey during the project

The project Euronet-PBL started its work by producing case studies and interview material on practice-based learning opportunities and on the cooperation between universities and enterprises. Below, some brief remarks are presented on the role of the studies as a basis for mutual understanding and for common conclusions.

- The role of common methodologies for local activities: In order to create a basis for trans-national and cross-cultural dialogue, the project chose a strategy that was based on case studies and stakeholder interviews based on common guidelines. In this context the use of common evaluation criteria and a common workshop format was foreseen to get an overview of the success factors, eventual problems and the views of the different parties involved.
- The role of case studies and interviews: The research partners have firstly produced information on students' projects and learning activities (*"micro cases"*). This picture was complemented by interviews with (other) students, company representatives and university representatives, who were directly involved in practice-based learning arrangements. In addition, the study programmes were analysed to clarify the preconditions for cooperation between universities and enterprises (*"macro cases"*). This provided the basis for discussions in evaluation workshops and data for comparative analyses.
- The role of evaluation workshops: The partners organised evaluation workshops as joint self-evaluation events with students, enterprises and university representatives. The aim of the workshops was to stimulate a discussion that covers the whole process of the cycle of practice-based learning. For this purpose the partners used a common set of criteria and an iterative discussion process. The participants firstly agreed on the weighting of the criteria (*preparatory measures, implementation of practice-based learning, immediate follow-up, further effects*) and then gave their individual ratings. The external moderator then chaired a debate in which the participants were challenged to present their grounds and consider alternative positions. In this way the workshops proceeded from individual statements towards gradually emerging common conclusions (without the need to reach consensus).
- The preparation of the comparative analyses: The empirical studies already made it clear that the comparative analyses should not give an overemphasis to national Higher Education policies or to the European policies. Equally, it was clear that the comparative analyses should link the university-specific starting points to wider national and European contexts. To meet these requirements the comparative framework was processed with several discussion rounds to give a proper picture of country-specific boundary conditions, the role of European interventions (in particular the Bologna process) and the shaping of university- and faculty-specific traditions. In this way the comparative analyses led to a European

group picture of countries, domains and patterns of practice-based learning.
- The preparation of a common (developmental) framework: The project aimed to prepare a common framework for promoting the quality of practice-based learning. Yet, in light of the diversity mentioned above, the project found it difficult to formulate common recommendations. Yet, the interest to identify and promote initiatives that strengthen practice-based learning called for a common framework. At the final phase it was possible to use the common process model as a core structure and some selected cases as illustrations of good practice. Then, with reference to the cases, it was possible to identify common working issues and propose recommendations.
- The preparation of the common toolbox: The idea of a common toolbox was closely related to the idea of a common (developmental) framework. There was a need to bring together a set of tools and instruments for promoting the quality of practice-based learning. Yet, it required several discussion rounds to reach a format that helps users to specify a range of tools to be used at different phases of work. The solution was found with the help of the common process model that is the foundation for a Moodle application.

Looking beyond the Euronet-PBL project

So far the brief remarks have characterised the internal development within the Euronet-PBL project and the learning experiences made by the project partners. However, when revisiting the working documents and the final results of the project it is possible to see that the project had a very special approach to European cooperation and that this resulted in very specific messages regarding 'European added value' of the findings. This needs to be reflected in light of the contributions that have been selected in this book publication. Below, we will present some reflective commentaries on the contributions to draw attention to such 'key messages' that have wider implications.

Therefore, we pose the following questions for reviewing the findings and the learning experiences:

- What have we learned of the comparative analyses? What are the key messages for future European cooperation activities?
- What have we learned of the empirical analyses? What are the key messages regarding common European recommendations?

- What have we learned of the evaluation activities? What are the key messages regarding use of evaluation methodologies?
- What have we learned regarding conflicts and tensions at the level of universities and faculties? What are the key messages regarding specific university policies?
- How can we summarise the contribution of the project – and intellectual work arising from the project – as contributions to European policies?

Messages arising from the comparative analyses

The comparative analyses of the Euronet-PBL project gives a picture of the differences between the participating countries and the differences between universities, the domains in question and the models for organising practice-based learning (from work experience placements to research-intensive study projects). Based on the mapping of differences and some key messages arising from the empirical studies, the comparative findings provide a European group picture. This gives the basis for the questions on the role of European policies and for drafting common recommendations.

However, when looking more closely at the comparative approach, it is worthwhile to make some specific remarks:

- The comparative analyses were not based on country-to-country comparisons or domain-to-domain comparisons. Thus, the study programmes were not considered as mere exemplars of national higher education systems or domain-specific developments across Europe. Instead, they were recognised as specific cases to be explored.
- The study programmes were analysed both from the perspective of the institutional background and from the perspective of implementing new European policies. This provided insights into tensions, changes and to developmental choices.
- The practice-based learning arrangements were analysed both from the perspective of institutional goal-settings (how keenly they were integrated to studies) and from the perspective of autonomy of students (freedom of choice). In this way the comparative analyses drew attention to reference cases (stronger ambitions regarding integration and students' involvement) and to parallel cases (weaker emphasis on integration of studies and on students' participation).

In this way the comparative analyses brought forward different overviews in which the study programmes could be seen in different sets of boundary conditions (country-specific developments, domain-specific developments and strategic choices regarding the role of practice-based learning). This provided a new basis for drawing conclusions – identification of good practice and presenting recommendations according to the goal-settings of the universities in question. If the universities had similar ambitions as the reference cases, they could follow the messages arising from the analyses. If the universities were not in that position, they could specify why they gave a weaker position for practice-based learning.

Likewise, the comparative analyses have brought the 'European dimension' of the project results into discussion by posing the following questions:

- Can the project findings be presented as direct feedback on the implementation of the Bologna process or as a basis for new European-level frameworks?
- Can the project data and empirical findings be presented as evidence on national regulations that can be harmonised with the help of transnational policy dialogue?
- Can the project findings be presented as evidence on strong university-specific conventions or guidelines that can be used across different domains?
- Can the project findings be presented as evidence on strong domain-specific models of conventions that could provide a basis for "European standards"?
- Can the project findings be presented as evidence on strong organisational arrangements that can be highlighted as generic models for good quality?

The project, however, had to give answers to all these questions. In terms of how the project's findings could provide European added value and contribute to common developmental efforts, the answer was as follows:

"… for a European project it is possible to present a comparative picture, in which the background factors, relative success and evolutionary prospects are analysed. In this way the country-specific and domain-specific developments can be seen as evolutionary elements of a European group picture."

Messages arising from the empirical analyses

The project presented an overview of students' projects in three participating countries (Germany, Denmark and Slovenia). Here, it is worthwhile to note that the cases represent somewhat different arrangements and that the universities have somewhat different policies regarding the role of practice-based learning. Below, some key points are addressed with reference to German and Danish cases. These exemplars draw attention to the process of finding appropriate tasks and to the students' capability to respond to the enterprises' needs.

German cases (Master level, vocational teacher education)
- Student A (male) made observations on teaching/training styles of teachers at school and trainers in the workplace. He also observed learning styles of apprentices at school and in the workplace. In this way he identified gaps and mismatches that could be taken up in the regular cooperation between the vocational school and the enterprise.
- Student M (male) used a standard tool (the QEK-tool) for analysing costs, benefits and quality of apprentice training at an enterprise. With his analyses he produced a picture of good practice and he completed the results with his individual questionnaires.
- Student S (female) analysed the needs to change the training plan of an individual company due to changes in the national training regulations. Her analyses identified that the quality of training was good and that the changes (required from all enterprises due to the regulations) had already been implemented in the company-specific arrangements.

Observations on **Danish cases** (Master level, interdisciplinary management studies)
- Student P (female) had the task of observing the communication culture in a male-dominated industrial company with a male-dominated blacksmith culture. The company had introduced autonomous group work and there was no evidence of how the groups work. The students' report (to her surprise) was considered as valuable and fair documentation and she was invited to work on her master's thesis at the company.
- Student L (female) was assigned to a consultancy company without a clear project task. Thus, she was first employed as a secretary for a group of consultants. Then, an agreement was reached that she should evaluate some training courses. Thus, her reporting (via

learning logbook) combined the observation on the group work and the evaluation results of the company. This case gave rise to discuss the need to formalise the agreements on students' tasks with a proper contract (see chapter 1 in this book).
- Student S (female) was assigned to a waste management company to work at the recycling and energy production plant. In her case the communication on her placement was minimal and there had been no clear task for her. Thus, she had to use her own initiative. It appeared that the plant had no procedures for receiving visitors and presenting the processes to them. Student S developed the model and it was implemented during her stay. This case also revealed the need for proper contracts for such arrangements (see chapter 1 in this book).

After presenting the secondary analyses of the individual cases the lessons from these cases were examined with the help of the common process model. Thus, the material was scanned again to find answers to the following questions:

- What can we learn from these cases to improve the preparatory measures?
- What are the lessons for improving the implementation and support during the process?
- What can be improved regarding the finalisation and follow-up measures?

It is worthwhile to note that these conclusions are not presented as general recommendations but as working issues. This approach follows the conclusions of the comparative analyses: the needs for improvement and the working issues are related to the strategic choices on the role of practice-based learning. This could lead to discussions like 'application as part of the learning cycle', 'increasing the research-orientation', 'finding balance between individual and collective learning' and 'the emerging model of Higher Apprenticeships'.

Working issues for further development

The comparative analyses and the empirical analyses bring into play a diversity of models and further differences in the implementation. Therefore, the conclusions for developing practice-based learning have not been presented as general recommendations but as working issues for further development. The analyses provide a picture of where the universities now stand with their current practice. How to develop the role of practice-based learning in light of the identified *working issues* is dependent on their strategic choices.

- Application of knowledge is part of a learning cycle. As we can see from the studied cases, the students gained a better understanding of key challenges in their profession and in real life contexts. Thus, without transfer of their knowledge into a context of application the students would hardly reach a deep understanding of their field of study. This has been emphasised by Henriksen, "The ability to learn theories and methods *and* the ability to understand and use theories and methods are far greater when *application* is part of the university curriculum" (Henriksen 2011, p.15). The chance to combine professional learning with scientific learning is much greater when high quality *practice-based learning arrangements* are integrated into the university curriculum.
- More research-oriented and more closely integrated arrangements. Some of the studied models were mere work experience placements. Some of the models provided opportunities for practice-oriented studies and analyses. Some of the models included both elements. In this respect the future role *of practice-based learning* has to be discussed more thoroughly. The feedback from students suggests that more practice-based *and* research-oriented learning should be provided across the study programmes. When this is achieved, universities and the hosting enterprises will also benefit more from the cooperation.
- Individual versus collective learning. So far most of the practice-based learning activities are carried out as individual students' projects with *ad hoc* agreements with the host organisation. Arrangements in which an annual project is agreed on the basis of a framework agreement between the university and hosting organisation(s) are still exceptions. (In the Euronet-PBL project such a model was represented by Sabanci University, Istanbul, with its Company Action Projects.)
- Making further use of the students' results. From the host organisation's perspective the students' findings can be seen as contributions to a pool of company-specific knowledge. From the perspective of the faculty, the students' projects can be harvested into a wider pool of knowledge on partner enterprises. These working perspectives open new prospects for university-enterprise cooperation.

- The role of practice-based learning in accreditation processes. So far the accreditation processes of study programmes in Higher Education have primarily paid attention to the scientific contents and on the academic curriculum elements. However, one of the aims of the Bologna process is to strengthen the employability of university graduates. Therefore, the role of practice-based learning in the curricula merits further attention. In this respect the Euronet-PBL has provided basic analyses and developed an evaluation concept to support a quality debate on practice-based learning.

Messages arising from the evaluation activities

The Euronet-PBL project used evaluation methodology encompassing workshops organised by the national partners. Below, we firstly present some remarks on the national evaluation workshops and then proceed to the secondary analyses.

The evaluation workshops organised by the Euronet-PBL project have greatly enriched the picture on the functioning of practice-based learning. They have also revealed diverse challenges and working perspectives for future measures.

The German studies and workshop discussions gave a picture of a deeper integration of students' Practicum projects into their other studies. The discussions also indicated that there is a growing readiness to link the *Practikum* projects to the needs of companies on new knowledge (on the quality of apprentice training).

The Turkish studies and workshop discussions referred to a fundamental integration of *Company Action Project (CAP)* as the overarching framework of the final phase of the MBA programme. The discussions also identified the intensive cooperation of the hosting companies and the student teams and the openness of the companies for the new knowledge and insights proposed by the student teams.

The Danish studies identified a set of contradictions (between national funding policies, university traditions and faculty-specific arrangements) that have blocked the development of *Praktik* placements in the engineering studies, However, in a parallel interdisciplinary study programme it has been possible to develop practice-based learning as part of a university course in field studies.

The Norwegian studies and workshop discussions identified the role of *Praksis* placements in the vocational teacher education as an opportunity to gain experiences with neighbouring occupations that belong to a common vocational subject cluster. Yet, the integration of the placement with other studies has not been strong. The workshop helped the participants to consider the importance of such placement in a new light.

The Irish studies and workshop discussions referred to the fact that the *Cooperative Learning Placements (COOP)* of the University of Limerick have been consolidated as a mandatory element of Bachelor studies. However, since these placements are implemented by a special service department, the integration of practice-based learning with studies is not strong and the involvement of faculties is relatively marginal.

The Slovenian studies and workshop discussions identified the role of *Praksa* placements as a mandatory part of the Bachelor studies and the particular possibilities that were related to the study programme, Social Informatics. This study programme paid special attention to the integration of the learning in Praksa placements to the studies and the companies showed a willingness to support this development.

By using the common process model it is possible to draw attention to different phases of practice-based learning arrangements (preparation, implementation, finalisation, follow-up). Here, the examination of relative strengths, relative weaknesses and contradictory ratings (across different workshops) opens new possibilities for learning from each other.

Messages arising from studies on particular university policies

The Euronet PLB project also presents insights into the question, how practice-based learning and professional development of students are valued by specific university policies. The project specifically refers to particular Danish and Irish universities, but the discussions could be brought to a more general level.

In the Danish case it was clear that the funding model was a problem. The university would not receive any student grant from the ministry, if the practicum was called "praktik" because of an old tradition stating that praktik is happening outside the university, and consequently the university should not be paid for it. This is maintained even if the university provides supervision, evaluation and pays the external examiner a fee for attending the exam at the end of the semester. This has resulted in a lot of frustration among teachers and programme mangers, as supervision and evaluation/exams are costly but the practicum semesters do not generate any revenue. This problem is dealt with in two ways. In some programmes the students are asked not to participate in any practicum arrangements and in other programmes the practicum is simply renamed. Then it becomes 'gathering of empirical data', 'an extended company visit' or any other fancy name to avoid using the forbidden word 'praktik'.

The Irish cases pose the questions, to what extent the hitherto presented arrangements are sufficient to train 'well-rounded professionals' (Lave and Wenger, 1991).

Both cases, the Danish and the Irish, address specific arrangements for practice-based learning in particular universities. However, they do not merely concentrate on selected study programmes or placements. Instead, they take the issue 'practice-based learning' as a central theme and pose the question for the whole university education. In this context they take note of the fact that the pedagogic reform movement for problem-based learning (PBL) has long been influential in both universities. At Aalborg University there is an overarching university policy to promote problem-based learning throughout the university curricula. In this respect it is somewhat surprising that the role of practice-based learning is controversial (for political and economic reasons). At the University of Limerick there is a strong commitment to the mandatory co-operative learning placements in all Bachelor programmes. However, the analyses of the project raise questions on the integration of these placements to the subject studies.

In light of the above it is not surprising that both cases take the discussion to a deeper philosophical level – to questions on the role of 'application' as a necessary precondition for academic learning *and* professional development. Both cases acknowledge the commitment of the said universities to core philosophies that recognise this basic principle. Yet, they raise critical questions, to what extent this principle has been followed in the valuing of practice-based learning at the level of study programmes.

Conclusions - Contribution to EU policies (and cooperation)

One of the motives for starting the Euronet-PBL project was the observation that the role of practice-based learning has not been clearly addressed at the level of higher education policies. So far the development of the European Higher Education Area has been promoted mainly by the following activities of the Bologna process:

- Introducing common structures for degree programmes (i.e. the Bachelor/ Master-structures) throughout Europe

- Introducing a common framework for credit transfer (the ECTS) throughout Europe,
- Introduction of common procedures and monitoring networks for quality assurance both at the national and European level,
- Promotion of curriculum development with the help of common guidelines in selected academic domains (the Tuning project and affiliated networks).

In general, the developments mentioned above have been launched on the basis of a broad intergovernmental and inter-institutional consensus. However, even if the relative importance of practice-based learning can be argued with reference to key documents of the Bologna process, there is no clarity of how to promote practice-based learning across the emerging European Higher Education Area.

During its work the Euronet-PBL project could find major differences regarding the scope, status and recognition of practice-based learning in the study programmes. In some universities there were common policies (e.g. in the University of Limerick and the University of Ljubljana), but in most partner universities the role of practice-based learning was decided on the basis of domain-specific guidelines or on the basis of faculty-specific decisions.

In light of the above the Euronet-PBL has sought to identify:

- patterns for integrating practice-based learning into existing study programmes,
- common quality criteria that can be used for analysing the strengths and weaknesses of current arrangements,
- possibilities for making the learning processes more transparent (within the curricula) and the evaluation of learning results more coherent (across the diverse domains) and
- possibilities to promote new developments with the help of common comparative frameworks and developmental guidelines.

Consequently, the empirical studies and the evaluation workshops of the project have been used as a basis for dialogue between the stakeholders that are involved in the practice-based learning arrangements. These discussions have highlighted the success factors, potentials and relative weaknesses of current arrangements. In this respect the comparative analyses have produced a European group picture of practice-based learning (with a focus on country-specific and domain-specific features and on different organisational models).

This has been taken up in the way that the project has formulated conclusions. Instead of presenting universal recommendations the project has drawn attention to the universities' own choices – to what extent they value the integration of practice-based learning and academic studies. The project has provided comparative overviews, lists of working issues and a common toolbox. In this way the project has indicated the direction – to learn from exemplary cases and to learn from each other. Thus, the project has been cautious, not to formulate quasi-universal generalisations that do not take into account the starting points of diverse universities and their boundary conditions for integrating practice-based learning into study programmes. However, if such integration is considered appropriate, then it is clear that the faculties need to engage themselves in the preparation, support, assessment and follow-up of practice-based learning. This can be emphasised as a common result and as a key conclusion arising from the project.

References

Henriksen, Lars Bo, 2011. *PBL and the Question of Real Learning*. Berlin, Germany. ECER 2011 - European Conference on Educational Research.

Kämäräinen, Pekka & Deitmer, Ludger (eds.), 2012. *Promoting practice-based learning in European Higher Education Area – Analyses, Frameworks and Tools for Development.* Evaluation Europe Handbook Series. Volume 6. Bremen.

Wenger, Etienne & Lave, Jean, 1991. *Situated learning: legitimate peripheral participation.* Cambridge. Cambridge University Press.

About the authors

Lars Botin
  Associate professor, PhD
  Department of Development and Planning
  Aalborg University
  His main research fields are philosophy of technology, cultural assessment of technology.

Ludger Deitmer
  Senior Researcher, PhD
  Institute of Technology and Education (ITB),
  University of Bremen
  His main research fields are in comparative VET (vocational training and education) research and design of innovative learning environments.

Lars Bo Henriksen
  Professor, PhD
  Department of Development and Planning
  Aalborg University
  His main research fields are technology management, engineering practice and engineering education.

About the authors

Pekka Kärmäräinen
Senior Researcher
Institute of Technology and Education (ITB),
University of Bremen
His main research fields are in comparative VET (vocational training and education) research and design of innovative learning environments.

Lone Krogh
Associate Professor, Head of AAU Learning Lab
Department of Learning and Philosophy
Aalborg University
Her main research fields are university pedagogy, educational policy and academic staff development.

Mogens Pahuus
Professor
Department of Learning and Philosophy
Aalborg University
His main research fields are philosophical anthropology, life-philosophy and aesthetics.

David O'Donnell
The Intellectual Capital Research Institute of Ireland
His main research fields are intellectual capital, e-learning and critical management studies

Ulla Thøgersen
Associate Professor, PhD
Department of Learning and Philosophy
Aalborg University
Her main research fields include phenomenological philosophy and learning theory.

Merete Wiberg
Associate Professor, PhD
Department of Education, Aarhus University
Her main research fields are philosophy of education, theory of learning and education

Jörg Zeller
   Associate Professor, PhD
   Department of Learning and Philosophy
   Aalborg Universit
   His main research fields are applied philosophy, logic of practice, social ethics

Johan Askehave
   Research assistant, BSc
   Department of Development and Planning
   Aalborg University
   His main research fields are energy planning and sustainable energy systems